Settings

Also by Tim Allen

Texts for a Holy Saturday (Phlebas, 1995)
The Cruising Duct (Maquette, 1998)
A Panglossian Sequence of Little Riots
    (in the anthology: In the Presence of Sharks) (Phlebas, 2006)
Sea Ex/Change (artist's book edition) (itinerant, 2007)

Don't Start Me Talking (co-edited with Andrew Duncan; Salt, 2006)

TIM ALLEN

Settings

To Chris & Jen

from
Tim / Christmas 08.

[signature]

Shearsman Books
Exeter

Published in the United Kingdom in 2008 by
Shearsman Books Ltd
58 Velwell Road
Exeter EX4 4LD

ISBN 978-1-84861-006-4
First Edition

Acknowledgements
Earlier versions of Sets 31–38 appeared in *Tremblestone*.

CONTENTS

for Louie (born 19-9-07)

"... there cannot be a poetry of pure saying; the saying must exist in the said, as ghost to its host."

—Robert Sheppard (The Poetry of Saying)

TRIAL SETTING

I do not subscribe to the idea that the eye breathes

The eye breathes

I subscribe to the idea that the eye breathes

The breathless eye

Do not subscribe to the idea that the eye breathes

An eye breathes

Subscribe to the idea that any eye breathes

Breathless eye

The idea that the eye breathes

Eye breaths

A jury's say-so scribbled out doodle and paper aeroplaned an erased wig

Set 1

Elves as I was are not strong enough to do the heavy labouring required to get this gleaming monster on the road to the Earls Court Motor Show before I vomit fish cakes on the bus home from the Boat Show. JCBs are difficult to drive and get dirty quickly it doesn't come off ever. Decisions decisions who's turn is it to rain today who's going to scat sing the phonemes and what shall we put in the hangman's lunchbox no we gave him that yesterday? My psychic judge pops up again he must have a love-hate relationship with every accused wretch popping up before him but this time he's telling some wretched company what they can and can't put in our water to make us wistful. The Contemplation Exhibition visits this very town you can witness *with your very own eyes* how the twins Imagination and Luck are not just not identical but don't even have the same father.official though not famous

Talking about writing about football with off the mainland referee. At Argyle I countered Norman's constant referring to past particular games against so and so on such and such a day when the weather was this or that and the score was one-all or whatever with my own cloudy recollections where all the matches just congeal into one memory mass. Everything is frightening, even language that arranges itself into silence. If a last phrase is removed to make the preceding phrase the last and the process continues until only the first phrase is left making it both the first and last phrase what claustrophobic line has the agoraphobic poet put his autistic arse on?

Eavesdropped dirt doesn't disappear it just gets dropped somewhere else but in my book that's disappearing for if as I believe it does the Eternal Return means that life as a whole is meaningless but life not as a whole has meaning and I give you the book of my life to back this up the results will all be there including any soft-hearted sophistic draws with whoever disagrees. If you think the opposite is the case where is your book of life to prove it and if you haven't got one then you had better start one pronto Tonto.

A brook sneezes out of the hillside like the type of person they call a small time criminal.

Set 2

The admiral's feet were so small that when his gran committed professional suicide by working in a laundry all he could do was refuse confusion in the claustrophobia of her slippers which she never had time to put on. A newsletter worth its salt suggests how to grate a great cheese. Stopping and starting in Greek with the patience of the ancients trying to sound them out of the picture but I'll deal with the downright myth of a new world later. The postcard I'm trying to write with a rock ready to hurl in one hand and a drunken tour-guide in the other has a picture on both sides it might be worth a few bob. The scene focuses not on *sailors fighting on the dance floor* which I thought was great when I was selling burgers to the buggers in Union Street and giving them stern lectures about their depiction in metaphysical art but on kids running with crystals lodged in the ridges of their trainers umm I've a suspicion that's Paul Simon. A tradition of geekdom propels us into using a kind of bottled-gas misery a beheaded man spouting poetry from his neck like a lifeless drawing is one of those *the posh can't be shocked* sketches for sale in a frame in a shop in the back streets where a glutinous flood of dodgy formatting makes you wish you'd been cheated or really had. The kind of low-down deception that brings you alive with indignation.

Don't put your trust in rusty sculpture either or revisionist disc jockeys who when at home fill their jukeboxes full of Bartók and bebop but no Abba. Talking to Steve and a lone drinker got up from his corner and starting talking like Steven Hawking Jack Hawkin' his Dalek voice towards the bar where an uneven conversation was already taking place between a barmaid who looked like a barman and a customer who couldn't choose between bottle or tap. It was like pouring motor oil on mashed potato. Of course the man wasn't talking about time and space and big bangs even though I couldn't make out a word I suspect he was talking about little bangs then a Screamin' Jay Hawkins tribute band walked in and all of us were instantly auteur.refugee cred

Shelf life. It so happens that in our culture some people share the same first name we take this for granted we shouldn't we should be more careful only when they share both first and second names do people raise an amused eyebrow I bet you you've noticed that too I bet you a fan club of your choice with all the fittings.

Set 3

The deeper you go the shallower the water is because the deeper you go the less distance there is to the bottom. This is very important and gets increasingly more important until it is so damn important that it is not important any longer. Having a party inside an advertisement the studio sun shines on the garden where most of the barbecue is taking place the garden party wives let their hair compete with the summer air for importance. Blood orange in transparent jugs of this and jugs of that. Paws paw hair for just a moment will you.

Inky-blue estrogens streak the steak by which I mean the steak is stroked by the *height of poetic inspiration.* A group talk a group play a group my god a moving group he is surely the son of a moving group. Pea coloured clouds in a pee coloured sky tug at slack harp strings. Cool looker chases the moment into a sallow teak shopping centre where there ain't no nature and an *only browsing thankyou* radical capitalist philosopher bites her face off at a temp calligraphy stall set up outside the Disney Store.weigh down in Dixie

Pan slid casually into his casuals. They tied his favourite causes to a burning martyr and watched the Irish in him flake off. Snails hop like rolling dice.

Can't help it. In the street a cat sat in the road.

Over the fence then over the wall then over the hedge then over the bridge then over another fence then over a car until the party's over the afternoon a queer collection of stamps you couldn't sell at the carboot just as you couldn't sell adults antique toys but now they all want the Etruscan gadgets. A huge yacht on the back of a huge lorry comes up the road into the district's spinning plume. All sizes no ages no grilled scarab no double-decker emerging from the subway disguised as a plain- clothes detective yet. This is no more than conventional buttressing it keeps you from smelling the candidate's rosette. Trapped under laminated surface of sea Pincher Martin is a set free pronoun with grazing rights.

Set 4

Because he fell up the stairs he fell past the stars. Putting the words there for a predetermined effect but not really knowing what that is going to say because until the words appear at the bottom of the page it is the bottom of the stairs. And the other way around always the other way round as if an air bubble in one ear was a speech bubble in the other. Bossy horse puts on a pressurised suit he makes himself do it he bullies himself he puts pressure on himself he backflips into the unknown.

We drove away from the scene eating blood and still not lost for words. Our gear is always on the other wrong way round on and on never stopping never reversing just going forever on and on the other way round then the other way before sideling into endgame free-fall. No vampiric excesses for us. No sexy aint half bad blotch before publishing our memes. A What's In Store For Us shop is an out of stock world a completely negative world not lost in this one and not lost on the other one either because when people move home the cat goes with them, usually. Not in the same sense of course not even sense times nine. In that sense it's more than a fictional device it's a way of talking about over sensitive identities and billboard tautology.

You thought though didn't you that an inner anthology of unused evidence would tell you the tall short story but it was just another abridged blockbuster joining up nowt to nothing nought to zero and the human condition glares back in dialect.

A peak-viewing gallery. Plywood clearly not what it isn't supposed to be or musical chairs. Empirically encoded imposition. Keep wanting to write *composition competition* not partake in one just mention it someone wrote something to the effect that you don't have to believe everything you think and I'd second that if only because it should be plainly obvious but obviously isn't. I tried telling some literature undergrads this when I visited them in a capacity they looked almost offended. He was Inspector Authoritarian and P.C Swelling Magma also. A good dream his job wasn't yours then eh steep plateaux? Escaped borstal boy breathless on moonlit steps to the moon.vitamin deficient Vietnamese highlights

Set 5

Retort. Love it. Retort. Could say it forever. Retort. Retort. Educationally speedy jouissance. Love it. Jouissance. Could play it over. Immediately on empty. Guess it. Unleash it. Love it. High thoughts sandwiched between thighs.

The soil burns. Cuddled in bubble-wrap.

She was jilted by the nexus of a wax figure's thigmotaxis. She married the next man available and immediately found herself emptying rubbish and glancing clockwise. All the king's horses and all the king's figurines and figures couldn't figure what they were looking for in that waist-high peddle bin gleaming like Excalibur they delved into muck and smell manoeuvred past stain and corruption as she liquefied herself in the sump of the plastic sack. The Co-op got back.

The Co-op got back to me. Sucking poison through a window. Another knock-on. Another knock-on effect of love language and law. If the *London Review of Books* fought Alice in Sunderland and Attila the Stockbroker won it would be because, if it is not too crass of me to say so, *it was a clash of symbols*. I'd object I'd retort that I'd have something to say about that forever but once co-opted what you eat is what you wear etc. It's a single cream applied to a double-entendre. Sweating shoplifter in a turtleneck jumpsuit pours the cream over himself as if milking himself. Self-love and self-hate marry in a little German church amid the little German hills of England.

A transitive set of opportunities. Think of a low little number and double it inaudibly as unmetaphorically a broken heart breaks killing me gracefully with faithful old improvisation and the busker who was singing it in American stops accordingly and says *blimey, blimey mate.*hateful systemisation

No vanishing guitars are in my arms. The Green Man entangled in mangled tape of Elvis's *Stalin Malone*.

An ambiguous quorum of anorexic thieves.

Set 6

There was only a war-aftermath in England everywhere else especially everywhere else in Germany any Japan left went on just the same with no side effects and a perfect France appeared in the middle of America and all the Russias playfully disappeared into Little Italy. Or inside every egg is a piece of suicidal nonsense trying to get out. *Dance dance wherever you may be I am the Lord of the* ripcord. The world was in ruins and it made great TV a boost to creativity and zippy image. A silver sword *Cut* said the Director a black gauntlet *Roll* said the Director a grey coat *Cut* said the Director and *Cropped windswept hair serialised just like lice ridden corn is the effect I want* said the Director and somewhere south of the sky it all worked for a little lad who proceeded to plunge a rusting ski stick down the throat of a fighter pilot.

On our own feeling special and lost like an orphan who is really the prince of the country he is lost in. A kind stranger picks him up and carries him across the rapids towards the block of flats where the lad is brought up as one of the man's own and there he grows up to be kind of kingly in all he does and people respect him without knowing why he marries the first girl he meets at college who happens to be the daughter of a disarming industrialist and they go on to have no children nothing zilch nothing comes nothing happens except the end of the dynasty in domestic secrecy but when they aren't holding each other tight they are as industrious as the flats are high.

Provisions for progress cascade from an occult distance. Pressure group descends on the poor bugger manning the tollbooth like a waterfall of ration books but an initial redemption comes in the form of *will you go out with me* notes like musical notes and after music comes maths then science and double history where listening to the lesson we learn that we'd like to get our own back on all the evil shits who've presided over us but even the mildest punishments seem impossible getting one of 'em who hates apples to bite into a russet thinking it's a pear. Our own come back to us but they've changed and are no longer ours alone. The obstinate fisherman has only caught a cold he sneezes onto a Henry Moore in Promised Land Sculpture Park where sodium light lit skateboarders don't look as bored as the sculptures. On a distant Dartmoor Debbie sings *the tide is high I'm moving on I wanna be your number one* in one ear while Churchill's speeches about beaches surge in the other.

Set 7

The shadow of a rattle rattles. The English papacy throws the fact that these are working beaches off the cliff-top. Enquire after their tricks and they box your ears and tell you you godda buy their box you open it as if it was a book therefore out flies a bedtime fable. Physical alienation puts a mental strain on the copyright company the managing director votes New Labour because he thinks it's an oxymoron he's wrong. Oh lay. The writing's bloody awful but the food is good and the girl-talk machine-gunning the tropes is infectious. The seedy theatre breathes in-and-out with the human tide and private eye in the shadow of the theatre is on my side which is good because he's got more legs than Weymouth Pier had the last time I looked.

Quintessential trivia. She kissed him he said he wouldn't wash for a week he saw her just before the week was up she smelt his feet from ten feet away so never kissed him she never ever kissed him again. We don't learn our lessons but at least we're on the register. Allegiances to music and fantasy marry on an imaginary day and they walk down the aisle as fantasia plays through its plot of how a sharp working girl and dumb princess swap jobs for a TV series the congregation is made up of one-time courting couples who ended up in court before coming together reunited by cultural bon-bons. This contemporary body is *contained of* sold council house stock no room in the inn for dolls in doll's houses even bulimic love-bitten Toby jug is *contained of* a gumshoe character alighting from a tram which ran a tramp over.lunch hour circumcision

Solo creative force cast a shed of doubt in the collective garden. The promises of an after-life were given too early they had a disrupting influence on machine-shop camaraderie. Recreational muse witnesses a lonely consummation on the commons. Red Cross certificate turns out to be non-applicable south of the river. An accountant has some charming little abstracts of his wall at work on his wall at home. Ritual cramp dreaming sleeplessly of creative momentum freezes a lyrical sequence into endless rows and columns of coaches we search for the Argyle bus in vain the buses move off two by two to a jangle of spurs to tour flash new bus shelter shirts before they're desecrated by an arsenal of stink bombs and vandals' hammers. Don't ask!

SET 8

The brilliant problem with nuance is that it always belongs elsewhere. Take prog rock for example it failed not only because it lacked concentrated space in which the nucleic could explode the little things which turn man into music when played by excited citizens but by too consciously ditching three minute impermanence for double-sided permanence it unconsciously planned its own dated nature. Its nuances couldn't travel. This is not an attack it's been attacked enough but a pointer as to why it left itself open to attack. Insecure trade-off biro lyrics show us why the bored can sound-write interesting while those whose lives are brim-full with balance can only bore you see pop is obviously made of tiny bubbles of nuance each reflecting another bubble's world of bright tack sizzling grime respect down a gutter of suds carrying itself to the sacred river of against-all-odds joy. A chord imposes like a logo a tune prints into a vein. Deafening discovery of silence and desirous scribble don't last long but while it does it lasts and lasts.ladder riots across imperfect square

Mandarin has the mind that can make the following link but it is a facility he prefers to delegate to a poet: *a great range of serpents impatient with nuance take hours to split.* You are not yourself with such green information. The delay issuing your personality profile card from the first such machine on the first ever motorway-stop is the ticket to a whole new universe much like the old one in everything except the insect size details. The delay is not important so much as relevant. The peaks and troughs of songs replaced cats and dogs homes *umm* says the mandarin.

Sunlight flies into your eye like a flint chip. Nonchalant problem solver slips on what others stick to. Once enrolled in origami class bridge the span between fat chasm and thin temple desk with a blunt bit of wisdom then crash-land concord into the grounds of a rock millionaire but he's not there he never is though archery ranges and trained arches are so march through an arch to the cockney tunnel where a snare drum joins in as indicated on the tour t-shirt then proceed under said tunnel to *enlightenment with closure* in the form of a large child a child so large in fact that mountainous does not describe him a pitch plus pavilion almost describes him and I could go on almost describing him thus until you forget how at large this child is but I could never forget. Normal sized children drift into an inlet where an outlet sprays them with effluent.

Set 9

During the course of an average Mass a mousetrap catches a hippo quite roughly nine times and every time this happens the hippo is raised by force but on average not every hippo is caught some escape back into their crate. The magic moment in the Mass came and went as if by text—snap—a great weight swung through baptismal urine until it was parallel with what it had previously sloughed off to avoid becoming embroiled in unparalleled envy. The dummy had lieges in its throat but the smoking ventriloquist was *as clean as a whistle*. The serrated edge of heaven and the buttery curves of hell moved blankly like Elizabethan war. The guns were loaded which means history was loaded which means steps were taken to construct University courses and pass them. Breton's paradise became a trace, a footfall, an approved school.smart meaning impertinent

Mickey-taking affliction in thrall to rash scarcity touched on a reason to be reasonable. The radio republic in the dowager's blackout let syndicalists in on the archaic rules of syndicalism and and hell finally broke lose from the Earth and and evaporated into heaven before condescending to return for the flimsiest excuse of a scented pocketbook and and a charity biro. My father sawed through the secret of stone. The secret was it was made of milk. The things people say are set in fibreglass.

Uranium ultimatum town of churches not a mile from these synchronised swimming sirens in sulphuric order repeating the glitter of chaos in a pattern of golden A's is reordered by the reedy piping voice of a protestor *the Romans are coming the Romans are here the Romans are going the Romans have gone the Norsemen are coming the Norsemen have been and gone the reptiles from the treasury are coming their wives are cleaning on all fours their babies are thrown off the trail.* A weenie harmonica no larger than a buttercup and an inertial tram join up and buy a newspaper I mean they buy the Newspaper as a business and institution it will complement their strategic empathy the way a wino does a dinner party. Oi, cocktail waiter, wake up.

Hunting for plums in the plump haunt of the National Forest.

Set 10

Cherub cheeked tousle haired skinny French chap said be absolutely modern long before my granddad was born because he saw the same terrifying vision as Nietzsche: a universe in which bootstraps are knotted too tight by a phantom tom-tom grandmother. Arthur the Author's maverick tie alternative was readily available pop nostalgia for David and me and plenty of others too skittering like crumbs across the kitchen top. Bird's Eye froze Bird's Custard in that part of my head where the mouth played tag with a bubble-gum heart. Those stains are your eyes.

Howls from the arcade. Laughter sticky gumming from the penny arcade. Screams cascading from the depths of the penny arcade. Howls of burnt-out fairground flying from the penny arcade. They shamble but not for long they shall not shamble for very long. Crepe reveres the rippling nipples on the beanpole girl outgrowing cupping hustings oh my pop-up soul I'm reading Michaux oh bloody hell this is just incredible when I read stuff like this I want to poke Sean O'Brien's eyes out with Sean Bonney's pen then let Michaux's ants loose on Motion's tongue until it gags some surreal sense those two tarts are not real people they are cut-out cops and when they hear the howls from the arcade they cream themselves with ash and whip monsters. The sea hardens.

The irony is restored. The cancerous breast is sewn back on. A gaudy darkness struggles like a meal to make its way toward the silky countryside where perfume becomes smell. Mystics coincidentalise those they've never met so they may stiffen themselves against the Unknown Ambulance that brought back the body of the Unknown Soldier (déjà vu—a purely personal experience). The emergency operation welds strength to length a fist the size of a face on an awkward acne'd hackneyed knock-kneed boy sprouting up through tousle to attach his shy mask with a broken sting. When a male deodorant becomes a household name some truths become seasick on the land of their fathers. Irresistible old country was resisted retro cliché to cut you short on the way back to the future of the *feature film*.sufferpunk

An apt phrase got in first before anything it could refer to my own poet in my share of the shed used it my own philosopher in my share of the medicine cabinet used it my own government in my share of anarchism used it as sharawaggi support-system.

SET 11

The First World War. Silver. The First World War left out in all weathers loses its colour. Family trees snake down the church wall as island England flattens its past in a post-modern symphony. Songs of death and sadness flown across especially from America. The First World War in a mirror in an antechamber to a tree house on an island of silver in the golden sea. The hacks and paparazzi settle down for a long paper-cup night as a third world a fourth world and a fifth world all come back to watch the First World War. French saliva in German beer. Grey. Grey soldiers with their lungs in separate poems. The adverts explode yes explode between the airport bar and the bowling alley train station.

This Setting is a robot's nerve the smell of a corrosive literary theory gives it the franchise while a rough diamond honeysuckles your liver and bungs antibodies at a tough school of twist. The man on the radio said that the First World War was a just war or did he say it was just a war or did he say his grandfather was called Justin or that his mother was a whore I'll tell you this he sounded as stupid as I imagined he looked there was schooling there and flute-high accent it was quite believable that some out there would believe him. This compass is too steady to be working properly.

There is a gorge on the ugly moon in which a family looking plausibly like us can horde their unscratched lottery instants.obsolete prejudice

Lumpen stud swamped by radar. Cornflakes open at his corn-flower funeral.

A group of inaudible metronomes and an empty-headed propagator arrive at the party dressed as countries. They mingle with treasure-chests of bones teeth and hair and pull historians without any books. It should be the other way around but the sound of drumming remains after its message is lost—wasted energy in an aviary. An echo returns from a far notion. A train *rolls by* and either its carriages look like giant wafer fingers or its wagons are carrying real giant mutilated fingers chopped from some anonymous European forest. The train pulls into a siding where a kitchen garden of remembrance can't recall a fuckin' thing.

Set 12

As determined to be deterministic as he was determined not to be surprised . . . the old grouch listed both his crutches as a single missing crotch began and ended the novel as a rowing festival was dislodged from the collective mind of a very local bank a bank so local you won't find it in Acapulco instead you find that the minds of the young work in the same way as the minds of the old both are mindful of the black economy without actually pooling their debt but a middle aged man isn't spring-melt either. As Alice said, *I wana be elected.* Slothful monk descends upon himself like a wolf in nun's clothing the clerk in the employment exchange said *You aren't one of those intellectuals are you?* and this was 1966 on Portland.

Practising slammers competing in the courtyard. The warder walks along the horizon's tightrope. Rules of balance rules of gravity rules of the bank rules of the novel rules of the slammer and the slam break those and you break all the others your broken bones thrown to the dogs of religion that compete for the region where ambient tapes are recorded if not sold they hang about in racks giving off ambiance. It was determination like this that built this nation on the banks of a river called the sea. A coelacanth attempts to soothe a depressed contemporary yet even more at risk than private landslide therapy is publicly funded escapology from dodgy politician's dodgy lodge slipping into the icy col where it mingles with mineral watered sloans as the music stops for a mo. Novel novel is slammed shut and the dust composed of its characters' dead skin billows into our universe.humpty dumpty Trotsky face

The expressionist tried to make an impression and did. She's not obsessed with packaging it's just that she genuinely wishes to be a delicate forensic purpose. The past exposed himself to her then ran back into the trees. You're continuing with the novel then? No, but a book we read a film we watch a series on tv accompanying a Victor Hugo passenger passing through a Moby Dick passage through a miserable North-West passage passing through a passing thought about the before and after of Romanticism all crash out of the bush with that flasher like the blast from the Siberian meteor they say was bigger than ten Hiroshimas and stay there they don't disappear back into the undergrowth you don't bury the elegy. A young poet makes that first comparison takes that first likeness epileptically knowing that such knowledge exists as an undiscovered colour that will eventually unpackage him.

Set 13

My mother's fibreglass curtains and plastic daffodils ended the future of the 60s.

A net of letters in letters makes memory dazzle a rusty watch sweats on a wrist of ice a doll hums a tune when conversation dries up in the naturalistic novel. You must tell us to let reality in you have to tell us pull the cord drag the trawl travel up the river of the real again *talk to me go on talk to me* it's the latest phrase bounding on ahead in every script. So I ask you this with my head askew in that questioning way what are talk's siblings going on about? Robert Creeley was so relaxed in that chair on the stage I thought he was going to fall asleep he looked so comfortable and as if in conversation with him I slipped further into my bucket but then I was slipping back up into a marvellous awareness and sure enough the man was upright too leaning into his shadow and reaching for water reaching for lubrication his voice laughing at the surplus transparency. Meanwhile the electronic muse massages Duffy's little finger dummy.limekiln crazy football mad

One night way back I dreamed I was fencing I had just cultivated my first cloak-and-dagger goatee but I gave my opponent a close shave we kept on talking about the Russian novel that had to change school buses as we feigned and thrusted. My sword rusted, well it had too, it came after thrusted. I flew at him with my trust in the dream gone but fell from the extravagantly arch window of the story into the streets of Moscow below where I lay waiting for the ambulance in a pool of my own princely blood and Cossack excrement. I don't like using the other word I'd rather use the word *rust*. A golden beach straddled by an oxidised sewer-pipe on stilts the pipe is made of the same stuff it carries even the stalactites hanging into the sand are composed of what this tube has dribbled and melted. Metaphors act. Metaphors act as sun blocker. Metaphors I haven't met before save a life. The Angel Gabe slept in the metaphor all night browned off like crystallised sugar by a cowgirl called Angela with raven black hair and brown eyes wider than the prairies but in the morning a change of vest was as good as a rest.

An exhibition of rabid coincidences circumvents human nature at the theatre bar.

Set 14

The punk suffers his sufferpunk because when a writer is in a creative mood he cannot abide the material of others all so much air and fancy. Country music from the 20s inter-experience. A diseased manuscript goes public in the managerial sense as well as the journalistic. Swanking waves of freaks gone whaling but when it comes to bathing in wooden tubs and sinks they start blubbering for canals of milk. All the connections are made for you so relax for as long as you are not a writer.

The Scots have their own look particularly the men. Father McGarry signed our foreheads with ash then told us about Saturday night soldiers getting venereal disease succeeded in making the whole thing unpleasant the sniggerers stopped sniggering but the rest of us started. The eyes of the world say yes. C&W from the 30s gigantic unchristianed sagas. When the dancing club was privatised I learned to do the mambo in half an hour tops. Buy caps pin on my sheriff's badge and take my horse shopping in the very same street where I just bought caps but the horse don't say nothing he doesn't know what Lorna Doone really wants from either of us.rowdy transfer market

Maureen Lipman in that Jewish aunty ology advert backed by the guilt of Henry 8 enters the eastern cities chart I told you I had connections out west. Jack K sleeps under the bridge and dreams he's a retired schoolteacher in a presidential home for the elderly tearing out the daily editorials and being generally evil in the sense that the devil is generally evil. Unable to afford such a bridge himself he fords the river gingerly in the manner of my first wet dream when in the middle of the road in the middle of the ball game where and when we had to scatter from the cars I gripped the hem of an Annette's tight skirt tightly and jerked it up to wake stuck to the sheet like a dog. Might have been 14 might have been because I felt sorry for her when Sister Madeline dumped her from clever class because she flared-up hot when the fat red headed kid ribbed her once too often. Who else remembers that? What happened? Was her life really robbed of prospects because of that incident? My sense of injustice grew into a mystery. I believe the boy grew up to have a murdered daughter.

SET 15

There is always more to say. Tiring how much mileage there is left. We stop somewhere because we have to stop somewhere take stock look back smile sigh and sing an old song someone copied out for us. Clouds take a short cut through my head. A Queen Bee follows. A baby goes through my head I can hear its cries.

In his roomy mansion a self-made millionaire drifts from room to room but close-up his drift is a broken rhythm. He runs into the gardens to run from garden to garden breaking into a sweat finding an old rhythm recreated the way a writer finds a voice in a pawn-shop but now he's made himself this is a bored man with time to kill and no heart for anything much so much that there is never any more to say no matter how much pent-up energy sizzles in his fats. What I am saying here is that the writer and the human are never the same person for if it were that simple then in mythology the planets would always be at war with the stars.

A painter and decorator went up in my estimation when he worked out what the puddle that failed to evaporate really pooled. He was ex SAS he'd served half a lifetime pretending to be a mushroom. Revoke sleep. No other way out for a patriot.

The skydiver is the perfect subject the nomad is the perfect object.desert island discs

The present can hold very little dust mites of *time out of mind* it cannot hold anything made of light it perpetually leaks a séance. Diachronic synchronicity cuts a section from a Victorian terrace to reveal a control panel this is a common occurrence in children's serials. Jo public walks the dog into the nearby park every day in the hope of finding a body while a nearby hotel caves in, psychically.

The steaming gantry gleams through steam it must be engine thirsty Thursday the train coalface becomes the guard's van transporting me back mum was a detective agency lifting me up to verify a working station was still over the wall. Bullet hole through notebook. Unsolved cases piling up in the waiting room where The Toppers dance to piped Al Jolson without blinking. Blink and the world changes *before your very eyes* spring back. The trees dance but they dance alone.

SET 16

Corporations are statues statutes and statistics anything in fact starting with stat so that would include states. Chorus line audit numb mathematical rehearsal. The Skoda garage got through the first heat it was young and knew that the forbidden was not yet condemned to a capitalism in its duplicated teens. The on-the-game poverty-trapeze artist gazes at the trace of what she grazed and chances it. An abusive dad keels over a crew of mothers in dry-dock we've lived in Devonport all our lives we've eaten it shat it out and eaten it again and the statues gargle in the night I've heard them and in the *morn* the statues are worn down just that fraction.

The sea walks into the recruitment office and asks to join the Navy it sits in a tripod chair from Ikea upon a deep turquoise pile the window to the street is a porthole and the posters of the sea are a broader deeper blue than the real thing the sea is given a series of basic tests in which it snaps its pencil so is given a leaky stick to write in no more than a 100 what it thinks it can contribute to the Royal Service and if you think this is old fashioned you'd be right there mate right there sat with the sea you'd be surprised how new everything looks when you're young and looking in the toilet mirror as you wait for the results it might as well be scientology.missing an anomaly

Liberty is made of plastic and what's so wrong with that it isn't a corpse? DeCoy dUke verBally goEs fOR miDniGht swim is mock lifted from another of my highly technical works and you'd want to quote something else here I don't know what but I know it's by someone stolen from their home. I asked the boss for an anonymous Frenchman and he didn't even look at me as he looked at me, which is different to looking through someone. His secretary handed over a list of American poets and a handbook on how to change from an acolyte into an editor so I turned left turned right took the lift took the stairs rode the stares and the escalator past the Escher etchings. Not finding what I was looking for after all I went home locked the door drank half a bottle of Irish with hayfever pills and hoped never to wake without that quote. I woke without that quote. Capitalism would have saved me had it known I was there.

SET 17

Human interest is soap interest. The Mystical Union joined the tuck shop instead of the TUC the mistake was exhumed and exposed but remained stubbornly dégagé.

The liner cannot fit in the harbour the nose called the prow sticks into the harbour which is why it is a business nose. The Cornish harbour has only one sweatshirt and when this is being washed in the laundrette that sits set within the row of small shops and cafes near the water's edge the shirt goes on-board the liner and wanders shirtless with its sweetheart through duty-free. Animism froths up the register of voters who discuss their latest local freedoms not just in local listings but in two automatic internal memos. The sets smell. Star releases her sugars poses with fans she copies who copy her in turn her hair is blown across old fungus face of the fishing fleet. A coastguard flag warns swimmers that the forehead on its helicopter is a big one but it's knees-up in the sweetshop and feet up in the sweatshop. Incestuous ombudsman.

A road map of Birmingham and a timetable took me to Cardinal Newman with a book by a symbolist in one pocket and a notebook of poems by myself in the other. The cardinal took me to the refectory he was dressed in a short skirt and he swept the hair from his eyes everyone was smiling at me all those miles out of town. A riverbed and a battleship sunk into the southern hemisphere but not together.

West-end understudy buys expensive books of art-photography his favourite one is of scenes from working class housing estates whether in obviously hot or obviously cold weather. Sometimes the star turn has tonsillitis or migraine then the art tomes remain boarded-up general stores and off-licences because although the understudy has an understudy he doesn't understand diagrams he can't work them out. The three actors never meet. It says access all exoteric areas but just you try it it might well be the password but you try explaining it to rats hemmed in so high up the head girl's thigh their conventional growth rate becomes an unexercised ellipsis.militant Falkland phlegm

Dom Joly's japes are exorcised grist.

SET 18

Went to the Arvon Foundation to find I was on a slimming course the stand-in tutor put a transparency over my distended lens to cast a purple shadow on the crimson placenta. Steve cooked tea while Mencius mended a fuse and the ghost of some Irish ancestor I share with John Kinsella blotted animal christening dripping with dove droppings. Psychedelia had a namesake. The whole point of sailing to the edge of the known world was to drop a secret or two off the end not come back laden with bootie but you know how it is you know how it goes one minute you own a fleet of bottled ships and the next you own a chain of museum shops bubbling from the end of Magritte's pipe between somebody's lent amplifier and someone's borrowed exit.

I therefore open a random book at a carefully chosen page. It is a collection of near death experiences. There are no illustrations even for such an exorbitant price the illustrations will have to be pasted in from a different book. That one about music hall will do the photos are transparent you can see right through them to the actress on the other side so you turn over the page and look through her at the one you were just looking at it is the only way to see what they really look like.

I'm not just a traveller I'm an activist if I discover a baby born covered in cobwebs I go off like a security alarm in the empty shop to allow the poorly paid overworked assistants to go home a quarter of an hour early. Outside the museum door a sarcastic windjammer the size of the Titanic eases into a parking space where an ideogram slapped in yellow paint looks like an outboard engine.sea cadets mob a glider

One day there were seals in the estuary and a year later a Viking longship sailed up the very same estuary on the very same day we could hear good humour carried on the wind I wonder what the jokes were about *WW2 bomb unearthed in the boatyard sends a manuscript to Stride* perhaps. The lights in the Liverpool Tate go on and off until the cleaners, all mothers of Beatles, arrive. Then the lights come on and stay on. A ketch installed in the gallery suffers from malnutrition because the warders on patrol have been instructed to feed it on a diet suitable only for a small sketch.

Set 19

There's not only tritium in the Tamar but light pollution on the deserted MOD macadam on its way to the underground bunker lit like something out of a nuclear thriller. Everything looks different from a train we could change our politics from here I could put that right-wing fantasy to the test not just own the water going under the bridging loan but pass over to the other side without paying any ultimate price. From the train the school the train passes had its own station all along Drake could have slept his way round the world on a sleeper but accompanying us on that evening trip to Calstock was an obnoxiously lecherous rotting drunk Time Lord so far down the metamorphic line that his skills were reduced to masturbating in public like a caged polar bear his polar opposite wife however wasn't even compacted snow let alone depressed in dog-collar and trouser-suit she was in control and ready to lecture on the connection between the early days of the industrial revolution and landscape follies.veterinary pharmaceuticals on an assembly line

Tag-end of carnival the lads are in a canoe race are hidden behind the levee so their girlfriends stalk around on circus stilts putting them up there with the unobtainable cirrus. Mayflies flirt on the towpath. In the Community Hall pensioners hold a mini-olympics now this is the sort of utopia worth class struggle and personal sacrifice the winner at darts wins a cuddly toy the winner at bowls wins a bottle of wine the winner of the trendiest root vegetable competition wins a wink and puffed kiss from the little carnival queen almost unbalanced up there on her long wooden legs she could get him locked up for a very long stretch. A fish leaps out of the river and swallows a cow.

Short caves.

Dated couple fill in next year's diary with drinking festering lolling back and bed-wetting on ordinance survey maps but in their MOT wallet a supermodel's passport renews itself without having to double-declutch. I'd like to write a form of futuristic Dickens but all I do is describe where I live giving pointless directions to those who've already found their literary niche. From a petrol station halfway across a ten-mile bridge neither estuary shore can be seen. Is it mist or is it distance? Fill her up.

Set 20

Pay attention for your ticket. The spooks may zero in on the traitor but there is nothing astonishing in your unconscious. The very idea of spying is not clamped to the horn of its volition but to consciousness described as an atmospheric catwalk. Generations of volcanic wrong turnings and nerves on the buffers. Another railroad song shaped by the underground wind gives us a promising idea in 1896 but by 1996 because blocked synapses lack a quarryman's shelter it remains a good idea but the wrong one, sorry. The tramp living in the tunnel survived such convulsive violence in a tube only by sharing a suit of armour with jumpy rats and performing fleas and on amateur night it gave up the ghost of an animated Eastern European ogre frightened of its own strength so they all settled for the quiet life of *before you know where you are.*

Preoccupied with his own little worries the suicide didn't notice that Britney Spears was biting him. He couldn't even be bothered turning the telly off. Other people's ideas send me to sleep but my own give me insomnia it's not that ideas have their moment but that momentum has its own idea of where we should be going, existentially speaking. War doesn't even scratch him but it does destroy his country and his family. He welcomes war with open arms. He gets the erection in Berlin but doesn't come until Paris. A body is laid gently in his arms then some cruel busybody puts the idea into his head that the dead child is his. A helmet can't stop wobbling.

Lived in a one-bedroom flat for years married to a metal detector then when the metal detector died he exchanged for a maisonette which he addressed as Tree House. The archaeological site disclosed the remains of a medieval bank the home of the teahouse spider and the weight-lifting ant.appliance of science yawns unconvincingly

Don't decline look interested as if reclining antique is interesting the man behind the trestle picks it up and moves a lever a hand a dial an arm saying *look at that isn't it interesting in fact it's quite moving* and yes you are moved but not enough to buy so move on along a James Bond Annual a Do-It-Yourself Manuel of Hinduism a letter offering anonymous a new career in Flight Control signed *Wright Brothers*, wow, and the choke of smoke and swallowed billiard balls from a chatroom.

Set 21

Now that the lake is free of its turquoise and can swallow the sunspots the new family in the street ask the postman to witness their passport application. It was a real sleep not one of those pretend ones it was so real I knew it was the last sleep of my life I would wake from its lake and stay awake for (an) eternity remembering its deeply impertinent dreams of second-hand oracle following their signifying chain back back into as much past as could be scooped from my imaginary lives. The thunder flashed and the lightning rumbled. The rivets that held the water-tank in the attic together became embarrassingly unreal it was a substandard transubstantiation not one of those flashy Catholic ones.magician's assistant peruses Christian Scientist notice board

I am used to this easy chair in which the absurd becomes aware of its own precautions. A move from common sense to the institutional ritual moves for an audience of one. Have you come across the idea that there is only one of us but many billions of Gods the idea came from my feminine side. When I first saw the Spice Girls in that Really Really Want video looking like stereotypic post-apocalyptic trash babes I thought they were Americans in Australia not five UK lassies the shadows were too sharp and masculine. The Relate counsellor mucked about with the new computer much as if it was real lives it said print screen so she printed screen. The conductor of an avant piece decided to ignore the composer's instruction to represent an electric surge by splicing a woman priest to a male stripper he said *let's stick with what we know faced by a sea of blank faces*. The audience all wore macs. All stood.

The super-ego is a stones-throw from flesh. Mad journalist mimics his notion of a mad poet calculating the radius of a circle as easy as popping peas *when the pods go pop* and palpable fate is in the pagan small print not in the Christian quasars. Writing for example is simply simple thought following a complex flight-path e.g. a beagle crash-lands his plane in a cat's litter tray e.g. in a nest built where the cat can't get it e.g. the story of Adam and Eve in Eden is still stuck in the introductory chapter.

Navigation Officer. Architect. Journalist. Famous writer. Drummer. Special Needs Teacher. Sucking sounds. Lost Jockey would rather be a chess piece playing football.

Set 22

Sadistic dare to murder your godfather play I spy with his stepdaughter turn her into a goddess having a bath with a plumber then turn yourself in or at least turn yourself into a mirror a bathroom mirror at that one that tapers away from the human into a tighter and tighter tunnel of speleological climax. Grope without rope to where the cave caves-in on a stag night flat-fishing its way into the quarry's quarry told four times by foul mouthed medium whose tent is inflated with the stale breath of astronauts kicking through chicken feed. Winning the pools means being rich enough to buy a low gravity swimming pool filled with inaccessibly plumbed omni-possible short stories by Ballard at the deep end and atrocity substitutes at the shallow. The Feds feed you a line you go in quick you establish the Danelaw you get out again.

It was on the TV kids were asked *how can you tell that your fish is happy?* I can tell my fish is happy because he is smiling I can tell my fish is happy because he understands me I can tell my fish is happy because he hasn't a fort in his head I can tell my fish is happy because when he comes back from school he shows me what he drew I can tell my fish is happy because the man in the pet shop called him Happy I can tell my fish is happy because he's on the telly. They filed out of the creative writing class and one of them turned to her friend and said *we're screwed now then*. In the pub they all tried to sit next to the tutor.

Glimpse of deep space gives some idea of what full employment might be like. Dan Dare has his job and John Digby has his and everyone in the Mekong Delta is busy. Glimpse of internal space is what full unemployment might be like. I blew the pools win on buying a Paul Nash I hung its pale bravery from the ceiling as if it was a drying kite I never really looked properly I guess there was beach sky and a quietly surreal phoney Anglo war infused with the amateur faith of a boy photographed in his summer between the Cubs and the Scouts. Decades of filth and progress later a labourer makes sure he's on time on his first day on the building site a boot-deep swamp of sick yellow clay last week he was on a family holiday in a caravan but now he enters this tilting *staff* caravan the rain beats on the roof a man in the corner casually munches remains and reads a paperback the jacket illustration is a section from the same Paul Nash hanging from the ceiling.gonfalonier fly that gonfalon

SET 23

An eccentric logo a belly button in the middle of a toilet seat. Knuckle-duster in auction. Ladybird ladybird climb those stairs. Court martial shaving facilities for anyone on the streets this antipodean Christmas. Disjunction is where I get off. Coitus interruptus fillets a semicolon in the major colon. The show-trial of an uncivil civilian a semi-detached fibber who voted for Totality degenerates into posturing nonsense. Outlaws in the forest give each other love hearts but they drink from an improvised drain and their tracksuits are not part of the ecosystem. Every whispered endearment passing between these *causes without a rebellion* echoes across stuntman dales. They cosh the security guard who robed the rich with the skins of the poor with the full knowledge of the guard's shop steward who nevertheless refuses to unconditionally condone the action until they run him over with a container lorry.playing Connect 4

Uncircumstantial pomp. Kenny and *me* went on hospital radio and I realised that 90% of my poems are about illness butchery and death so I was even more nervous would this jeopardise the station's chances of getting the franchise then Kenny spilt coffee over my microphone I tried to tell him that what's said in a poem doesn't really matter you could say anything what matters is the formal relationships he didn't believe me but then he went a stage further in not understanding when I explained how the formal considerations meant that the anything that could be said was therefore not arbitrary. One school bus went to different schools it's how we discovered that metalwork existed and how each school had alternative words for fart and Jeff Nuttall that you could actually hollow out and use as . . . um . . . something else too speedily hidden it never hurtled the bus into the weighty limb of a mighty oak either however woolly the sad fictions in your head could *crackle into life* and *knit into place* you know how it works.guilty party fat after school thins-out too lately partly arty early

In the greenwood tree without any pocket money or Maid Marions to spend it on don't ask if it's politics in the cause of religion or car-bombing in the cause of macho antics as long as the boys with the dark oval eyes find their nano-second heaven is a synonym for hell followed by the sinful darkness of the medieval English forest through which two figures wind their way home from the pub it's Alan and Geraldine.

Set 24

Missile with the name of a country on it plunges into the sea while we wait at home like a geeky Marco Polo waiting for the Chinese to open up China. We wait like slaves waiting for Walt Disney to part the cliffs to part reveal a channel to take them as leasehold freemen to see one second of Tyrant the Wrestler's three-second pin. What are we waiting for? Could it by any chance be the slap of The Cantos on brochure blue their tingling massage message and dazzling gall? Yep!

Here's something else to think about while waiting what if we were sky high peaks gasping for breath and the last line of trees were pin-men threading their way through us? And here's something else what if a tiger arrived on earth clinging on to a meteor its claw marks still visible next day on the cooled rock and the next night this tiger watches the night sky for the arrival of an intellectual on another meteor this time leaving no marks on the rock and the next night the intellectual in turn watches the night sky as a thousand and one courtesans arrive in a meteor shower? A ramshackle hut full of shed hormones in The Gardens of Experimental Permanence you might be but you too can attempt indifference to your failure to live off the profit of the pretty exotics while reserving the plain little fish for unprofitable teaching. It's a gesture computer artists appreciate especially when the tropicals get all the fun and frill diseases in frolicking bubbles of art nouveau. What is it about Coventry we're waiting for hyena? We await preservative.interview over

Haven't seen him since Glastonbury '95 Robert Smith enters a convent as a criminal psychologist enters a prison but this particular psychologist is made entirely of sea horses and unbranded cure-alls. First the local police plant a dagger on Fat Bob and then the warders stab him with it then the inmates regard him with suspended suspicion as his blood issues from his torn abdomen like red smoke from a flare as if he is under water but he isn't he's just starving himself into swoon with the other up before the cock sisters. Finally he misses his train by voting Fascist in the mist the city looked like ghostly countryside and the countryside looked like a ghastly city so he must have caught the train after all. Since then I've learnt how to live without gravity but with a heavy heart.

SET 25

Engraved school bell given to wide-boy headmaster who did nothing but puff himself up pumping public money into bargain debased computers and foreign excursions for himself and his ego. Expert at confidently running on the spot don't blame him blame the gits who appointed him power is voluntary cowardice. Not bitter not even sad can't describe how I feel no words to explore this numbing neutrality. Like most of us he was made of eaten flesh but his suits were fractal our man looks as if he's just seen an angel but it was just a souped-up Ford Princess. Celebrity culture was already swelling away from pert towards swell when a clay-headed bad lad was bounced out of the Penlee School Christmas Disco 1973 for singing the wrong words to Sweet 16 something about *popping buttons.* Tim and Paddy Hooligan run into the tin-mine and close it down around their Tamaritan selves the only things moving now are multiplying nits jumping around ringworm like featherweight boxers sniffing *bring it on* to entropy too many other contenders about but the majority are bus station light fittings illuminating tatty tartan petty tat grim micro-oven with matching glam micro-oven gloves decorated with tart's trews worn by Canadian packs of playing cards smuggled from Cork to Bristol smelling like the herring fleet. It all swills around in there the alien orange lava lamp comes into fashion goes out comes back then goes on the end of a grave hoard itinerary to light a way through the underworld. I can see why Dalí was obsessed with William Tell.brother can you spare a diamond mine

A lost plastic comb became a metal one in my head it scratched away at scurf breaking skin and gouging into skull until it combed the brain and I tasted metal on my tongue. Now the final skim while the page is still wet for a writer must offer themselves up to these clichés like getting away with murder in heaven while original old gOD is too preoccupied with being up-to-the-minute to care. Meanwhile though it is connected the way cousins are connected by wills in the capital punishment capital of the world an article in the free advertiser's arts column features a forensic pathologist clearing a track of logic through urban scrub where you are likely to snag your ankle on the trunks of children who stopped growing prematurely. This trite testament to serial madness has a boss stuck on the motorway like an Adam's apple. After Bataille an open grave laughs openly and a closed grave eats silently.

Set 26

Scarcity in Utopia. A rare reference to Terrible Work gyrates about in a helium cloud coalescing with microdots of glossy post-language into the Mick Jogger Grinning Informally Galaxy. It is gone home time a lone shark ago in that parallel universe where TW sold out but didn't sell out and Mick had a little less to grin about. English youth cults continue to decipher alien signs more accurately than anyone else. Seasick cows stuck to whaling ship's rusting bulkhead communicate telepathically with the wider women's' issues.bet they got it all worked out bet it means something

Dancers limp from the club at dawn feeling like smuggled asylum seekers with no lighter fuel for their slick mobiles they go straight to their picket-line outside the *Words for Money* depot but the action has actually moved on to the warehouse next-door where drum-sets line up behind the fence like rows of imported cars in Avonmouth. The tilted snares snare the early morning glitter there is a blue set a red set a dark red set a pink set an orange set a dark blue set a lime green set a light blue set a purple set a white set a gold set and black set all silently symbolic on the gravel.

Predicted chaos sources more lonely figures of speech than we could possibly use. The petals of a wild flower on the waste ground where the fair annually sets itself up are a patient machine they gently enclose children then transmog' into metal petals space pod opening suddenly to hurl the kids into the sky where they become nauseous teenagers before the ride brings them back to earth vomiting as the imperial change falls from their pockets. Not everyone philosophises or do they?

Arthur Scargill sat looking the perfect image of Queen Vic not amused by minister's insults good gracious what an ungracious prick that Mandelson is I didn't just feel sad seeing Arthur humiliated I was proud to have voted for his losing party I've said it many times before nobody will vote for a party led by him but what does it matter there's more honesty and honour in his little finger than there is in Mandy's whole bunch of little pinkies so rage and regret churn and I wish I'd defended real socialists more and not been so quick to say *nobody's gonna buy that ancient rhetoric* even though issues whither when I turn on the computer and sneeze. The police horses charged the minors in a medieval dungeon.

Set 27

Fear turned me into a building society when there was no society but back when there were council houses fear wrecked tea clippers upon Irish pubs' sawdust shores where you could open up as many Royal Post Offices as you liked without clipping wings or attaching coded messages to scrawny not there pigeon claws. Fear colours sheets in the wind brown. I'm Mark Thatcher lost in the Sahara without his mum seeing a caravan in the distance carrying Bader's legs instead of Rimbaud's rifles.

The Babbage Centre is building on the exterior but inside it is an immense computer. I went there to learn how to draw and dress teddybear and make myself a sandwich and when I became the sandwich I had made I struggled into the body of a Babbage cabbage by folding teddybear's entire wardrobe into a file. It all helped. I intended studying undersea dust storms because graduating in obscure poetry would be too easy a challenge but I changed my mind when I read in the prospectus that a picnic basket in a Symbolist poem was an installation of 100 years of Sunday motoring. How did the petrol get in the basket did words put it in? I looked discretely at the problem and noticed how indiscrete this off-the-street poetry could be about almost anything pollution politics you name it so I changed courses again and found myself in the same class as Tom Raworth which set me thinking. Thinking about things is much like building a Tower of Babbage we wear Bob the Builder yellow hats the reason the UK no longer produces engineers is down to the preference for Lego over Meccano though once I made a bizarre machine with the claret and green I didn't know what it was but watched what it did until the battery ran out then used it as a dredger crewed by Vikings with flowing locks it dredged right up the Cam until one final bend steered it into a corner of a misty canal that looked to the crew like one of their very long grey gods going further and further into hoary old nowhere.absences in wartime register

You can descale a kettle but you can't take the limestone out of the cave boy. There is nothing automatic about automatic writing non-automatic writing however is pretty much automatic. I sat in my kitchen like a visitor half-cut with Devon Cream Tea and half-cut with some tipple called sourmash cider. An antihero sat opposite looking too clean-cut to be anti anything but we crawled in common with riddles only dumb kitchen appliances could solve.

SET 28

Debt cold echo of embrace. Oscillating crumb on chest. True winter will not abide the fiction burn only suffer endlessly like christ's christianity. The phrase *a wonderful itch in the left-handed ear* is not nonsense 'cause I said it walking with hands full of milk and odds and sods from the corner shop with an itch in my left ear only the day after I'd returned to England like a surrealist to Paris as the result of reading matter. Today the schools go back what's Peter Redgrove up to the stapled wad he sent me about tree energy still languishes in a box of dead letters the staples have oxidised. The Western Morning News has a photo captioned *the wide Cornish sky makes the small Cornish church even smaller* but that's how the picture was taken so what are they talking about? Also think of Leeds. I wanted to be the Captain in Boots & Saddles the action officer out there with the men and horses getting my blues dusty and nocturnal desert condensation down my barrel my sabre has tassels I ride back to fort back to front with the corpse of my flatmate draped over my horse whose rump is embedded with so many arrows that it looks like an Indian headdress. I am riding into Fort Austin to perform Texts for a Holy Saturday.stale insulin

Adults can look cute in adverts the family pet plays lead the children have supporting rolls as bouncers at a BNP meeting but the NME is being sold by Socialist Workers and a framed copy of the first Big Issue is auctioned inside the smoky room for the price of a one-bedroom flat in Exeter. Bigot bomb is thrown at kiddie Catholics walking to school in Belfast the English had no idea of the depth of dangerous hate the minority had to live with for over 80 years if I was the IRA I wouldn't drop the arms into Room 101 so it's a good job I'm not I consider Paul Merton a good friend over a pint I tell him *the medium is the message* was known long ago by spiritualists and he replies with the one about the team of eleven referees singing in the shower after their victory over the Black and White Minstrels while wearing tinfoil shorts.

At the wedding of Cinderella to Prince Buddha the confetti is made out of shredded prayer-book because it's a church *do* if it wasn't it'd be made from fragments of immanence. The streamlining of the Settings enforced by revision has a result similar to Inspector Frost finding the pocketed notes scribbled to himself have been laundered into indecipherable pulp by his woman who does.

SET 29

Pen rises into the sky as a rocket but not as a rocket writes into the sky more as an aeroplane drawn by pencil leans into the margin and that's not a contradiction because the rocket as likeness to the pen is on a different plane to the pen as likeness to a rocket. A similar situation arises with the need *to* sleep while not needing sleep *itself.*

Education has an audience.

Adjectival bigamy avoids the wandering administrator who as The Wandering Administrator has already caught up with adverbial bigamy. An Ealing comedy is showing in the Methodist chapel that stands on a concrete island amidst a sea of weed and rubble it is the tale of the sole survivor of an accidental remark whose only memory is of the day he received an informal education in media studies. Meteor impacts pockmark the cranium. Somebody interrupts to enquire if you understand everything so far so you say *yes* you do you *understand everything yes* they ask does it help to know the film was directed by Cronenberg and you say *yes that helps a lot thanks*. Coalscuttle shovels shuffled carbon on the cold floor of the coal shed scraping hieroglyphics that would explain, if anyone could read them, how your mummy needs sleep *itself* but doesn't need *to* sleep. The Wandering Administrator sits under the shade of a concrete tree to sell his Matisse forgeries.allotment dispute spills over

Polish greasily rots in desk grain but the limbs and faces of my imaginary siblings shine. My lanolin sister had an imaginary brother made of being made to join the Mile High Club by clouds of idiom in the form of clouds of tedium. In the in-flight film they don't let a prisoner take his dog to prison with him but they tolerate the way he turns into a dog over years of captivity. After many years of captivity the man-dog cannot remember his original crime but talking to the prison chaplain he gets the idea into his head that he was framed by a friend who went on to become a best-selling author so the prisoner writes a novel for the prison library called The Framing of Man. Unbeknown to the prisoner the prison chaplain is now a minister in a neochristian cult that has taken over the church you read about above. The plot continues to thicken. Took my drawing of a pencil done in pen and my drawing of a pen done in pencil into the gallery it was like taking your own food into a restaurant.

SET 30

The violence of American films is astonishing however crude extreme comic celebratory realistic gratuitous sexy satirical sick or serious they aim to be prurient entertainment is always the result they are like being like something without being about what they are like. Nobody is astonished by movies but moviemakers are tarnished little stoned creatures. Strawberry blond with moustache advertises for a reformed satanist and the lexicographer seizes his chance. Not too far off we can hear a town crier scream *the rain falls gently on the little town.*

The Americans make films in which everybody hates the Romans. Stupidity exhausts. There's no room in space we are going to have to go out there and make room. A tensile parade goes by every marcher reading a different mini Penguin sampler but they're marching to blasé jazz played by the tin man while the lion is on a phobile moan to Dorothy who high-kicks past scarecrow genuflecting in front of a pilot episode of Lost in Lostwithiel in which the pilot's swinging corpse from Lord of the Files swings dangerously close to becoming a Japanese film in which everybody hates the Greeks. Ingenuity exhausts.

Without the underlying structure of savage domestics the yankee empire set-up in the world's inner space would fall apart. A single herbalist failing night-school won't do it but a magician does not become sinister overnight any more than he is less scary after dark in fact like a hired clown he looks more sinister in *the light of day* kid's party when the cruelty of or towards the birthday boy is decidedly apolitical and wouldn't stretch back to the Iraqis conscripts buried alive by the US bulldozers which is too far back to haunt us now whether we believe in ghosts or not. Of course the Iraqis annihilated on the Basra Road can't come back because their deaths were just rehearsal whether you believe in rehearsals for capitalism or not because their souls were burnt to a crisp in a Christian hell so they can't haunt anyone though Tony Harrison who I'll mention again always looks scared.jesus was pasted to the cross

Speak to your warped floorboards coax them back call them names mock them.

SET 31

One the railway lines run from east to west the canals run from north to south because they sound as if they do. The railway lines are separated by a distance of anything up to a mile and ditto for the canals together they make a network that gives the country its character and though this network is on the surface it goes deeper it gives the land a personality. Two a hydraulic model of this is preserved underground in my attic it is electric but runs like clockwork. When I play with it I drawl my way across a big country I haul myself up mountains through a hundred steep locks I shunt coast to coast. Three as time passes the personality grows dark and in the shadows of the bridges that carry the railways over the canals indifference mushrooms into pigeons and in the shadows of the bridges that carry the canals over the railways empathy pigeons into mushrooms. Four the tiers of railway and canal play hand on-hand accelerating up into faster and faster laughter before toppling according to rules. Five when this happens in the scale model world the real world goes on in its own sweet old way and when this happens in the real world the scale-model world goes into a *mental home* where a high wall separates Amble Lane from the grounds of Amble Lane House. The grounds otherwise known as the Dawdle Gardens are exactly five thirds the size of the house itself. The half-cured inmates of Amble Lane House are allowed to lose themselves in the garden as long as they find themselves later in the house. Breakfast is early lunch is late tea is late supper is early but death has promised to be dead on the stroke of whenever. Everyone is happily half hearted because every mental process needs somewhere to call home. The spit-box and swear-box encourage competition and book learning.

But a brain too small to discuss things adopts the affectation of continual surprise. A bullet big enough to fit snugly into a big cheese avoids Chinese cities larger than London we've never heard of teeming with fresh millions on the banks of rivers too long and ancient to pronounce. Shouting over the incessant onomatopoeia of tinnitus drip intoxicated angels struggling with accordions help each other put on their parachutes. When he was an old man Pavlov hired a dog walker sometimes he paid them sometimes he didn't.glib echelon

Set 32

Chocolate people chocolate animals chocolate trees chocolate houses chocolate figures chocolate beasts chocolate shrubbery chocolate town. Chocolate buses melt in the cardboard bus station. Summer Goths in deckchairs expose pale skin tattooed with sculls serpents and family trees. Chocolate interim. Fake energy substation. Chalk.

Talking us through the equation the lecturer faces us turns his back glances over his back turns back talks to the wall talks to us talks to his world turns back faces us asks questions tells us an anecdote about a shower cap and a student says *Sir, couldn't that just as easily be a bathing cap Sir?* and he answers *No it couldn't you single animation frame.*

In the New Broom Garden Centre we all sucked-up to the racist boss. Flake advert trickery amid the English elms. Only the crumbliest flakiest floating voter votes like floaters never voted before. Torn parliament in the gorse.guilt alienated from ethics

The details don't matter I was in one room doing things and trying to get them right but aware that I needed to get out and go to a different place where another job was waiting so I had to drop what I was doing and make the journey to another place where I had to do something else and try to get it right then the imperative to return to the other place returned every time so off I'd go and follow the sequence through feverishly again. Only on waking did I realise that the room in both cases was the same room and the task was the same in each room there was no difference in any degree between the two places and what I did there or what I felt. As I said the details don't matter there was a crumbling violin in a carpenter's vice and a grocery brown female supervisor called Lisa Nightingale who just stood there frozen like one of those three-dimensional slices in a two dimensional field recently all the rage in videos but I'm sure that in one room she was in left profile and right profiled in the other. The legacies of our two civil wars were more evident in the repeat episode of Never Mind The Buzzcocks than anything to do with the history of British Pop.

SET 33

Miss Dalton said all my luck would come late in life now it gets later and later and I see her in Safeway car park quite a bit later in life herself at least I think it's her no longer wearing her lucky red hat. Cars full of people too full of the past are manoeuvred into empty parking spaces by lonely discipline. By the evening rush hour early morning swimmers have made fatal decisions. Discipline continues to twinkle on absent objects. Prohibition still has a certain attraction. Pensioned off language changes the tyres on a squat squad car into four cement mixers. Subliminal language meets Owl for depressing coffee. Babies crawl up trees towards the sky where there is no circumstantial disbelief. Shift-workers swarm. The secrets of seamanship.

Let at least one generation be free and immemorial. War has always fascinated me how ordinary dull civilised routine can be turned like a coin to nullify the values that exist in daily life by putting into practise those same values inverted. On my palm I see a past on Portland the ruined houses at the top of Old Hill whose ruination had nothing to do with war the rusting farm machinery extruding brown frames from the long yellow late summer grass we'd walk up that heart-breaking hill in peace in order to descend it in the dark knowing the way was lit because friends were hung burning from lamp-posts. I grew up in a place where the reminders of war were conclusive nods. The island isn't remote but the football players are they play on a pitch turfed with gammon instead of sod they have atomic numbers on their shirts and the number of goals scored is how many years they were away on the Russian convoys.gauguin

Proverb authority greater than any god.

Flushed with republicanism and superstitious about semblance a water snake sidles up because it was prophesied. Jiant gellybaby goes to the races smothers the steward eats the jockey and rides the horse off into the sunset of 24-hour telly. A large man is brought into the field-hospital he says his name is Olson and his wounds are not just his but everyone's *I've heard something like that before* remark's the army surgeon *Are you Whitman, Walt* asks the big man *No* replies the doctor *I am Mr. Antipyrine.*

SET 34

At night the brain is an illuminated formal garden but at day it is a reformed cult through which you walk naked without feet in your boots. The pretty fireworks of the barrage at the front drop into the wilderness-by-design at the back of the garden. Hide in mid 60s speculative fiction hide in the damp dugout of the one-sided wall away from the dry night heat hide your Elizabethan comic books written in Esperanto come out come out adrenal chase come out the rain is soft and your skin is grey-green.

Submarine over-ballasted with airfreight. Chemistry set put out of harm's way in the dungeon of a bouncy castle syncopates the classical collections of symphonic this and operatic that that my dad bought parallel with the Beatles to lift him out of the 50s out of the working class into culture and promise it's a natural and noble thing to do I shared in it by playing the Pastoral as I flew to the moon with the Byrds but I became just another shooting star illuminating nothing except its own flash presence.

Spirit replacement.tickertape

Frost. Wind. Downpour. Drought.

Godless ornamental rock garden. Devon without the rest of the universe. A resurrected Jesus walks round the olive groves like a zombie his eyes are soulless *the lights are on but nobody's at home* says Peter and apples fall from the olive trees. The country rocks the very end of the county an earthquake opens the graves but these are as void as the saviour's sockets. Someone screams in their sleep but an insomniac partner thinks it's a hoax. Genetic typos populate the theatre as nuns describe Limbo to their charges the way the Germans described to the Poles how they were friends of the people of Poland. Evil stealth is nothing if not consistent how different in other words will the last religion on earth be to the first? Walking to the post-box my mind was on Heidegger but on the way back thanks to Bill Gates it was on headgear then by the time I walked through the door I had lost everything except my mind I'd put it away for a rainy day so I took it out to put it on but there was nothing to put it on. Gravity and karma are not the same thing but poetry and compulsory education are.

SET 35

Never-never was always on the cards in blighty because by the time the Army got them home what had been unrelated adjectives abroad turned into slick twins christened Billy Properly and Albino Blake. A colourful lecture on the chronic internet talked of *an elimination unto the 40th generation* but it didn't say what of or how such symbol blizzards breed anecdotal complacency. I'm not convinced enough to care yet it occurred that the Beatles' split was the 60s split-hairs in cameo George went the way of gentle mystic spirituality while John went the working class hero way of the cranky millionaire's Tao and Paul took the long and winding road of liberal nicety and familial sense. Once their entangled hair on the sleeve of Revolver was untangled they grew apart at pace and had to climb steeper than spermatozoa to keep up with the promise of the past. Ringo joined me in the PLO but he rose in the ranks while I got stuck looking after the kids and their nail-biting smiles.

No information resembles the dissembling: Vietnam. The Merseybeat narrative progressively frees itself from history—windowless and on schedule New York approximates hermetic liberty. Nothing obscure in this obscurantism, friend, playmate. The tinker babies are dunked in a baptismal sheep-wash but only one will make it to Pope and unscrew Spartacus the flippery festive crooning mullet nailed to a cross on the pub wall to give us a rendition of Bowie's Changes. The first time anyone encounters this fish they attempt to harmonise more like husband and wife than brother and sister they come from different biological countries even though they speak the same lingo after all I'm a fully paid up supporter of stateside excellence in innovative verse more than most Brit mods but let's call a playing-card a convenient structural unit and admit that my anti-Americanism is growing like my hair in the 60s and my beard in the 70s. I'd like to perform this positive inability where it will not harm one real hair on one proverbial head but how far into outré space will I have to take it before Keats can kick-in. *I'm the rubber mullet No I'm the rubber mullet No I'm the rubber mullet.*neutralised questions

Meanwhile Mother Nature threatened my best friend. He wanted to be Carl Perkins but he became Moorcock's Elric Melon Bones rubber-stamping a Spanish guitar on a Play Dough Apollo 5 instead of eating all the potatoes on All Souls Day.

Set 36

Cover yourself. Cover-up under Howlin' Wolf. An Earth tremor says read Author A because it changed its life it became a World tremor as if the Wolf made a cover version of I Get Around and so could you. While on the other bloody hand what about Author B shucks I've never read B never wanted to never will you don't bother about brothers you haven't got yet what we've never read influences us more than what we have so cover yourself over and over again in a magic blanket do it over there in the corner of the squat stretch it inadequately over your aggression as if it was a recipe left for a reluctant cook. It's a shadow of the song it used to be a blues gone wrong gone bad like a bad dream that got worse gone from beauty spot to ugly blotch from dark brown oval to an irregular colony of cancer colour. Coronation mug stuffed with bruised wrinkled sky not just covered in it on what we used to call accidental purpose.

This return to what they call classical music goes through a negative series of partial orders so arrives so uptight in the real world that everyone else is relatively relaxed. The sounds can't wait for a release date to be immediate images they abstract the past into a passport photo taken in Pangaea. It's one thing being dustbowl philosophical in poetry criticism but what happens when this meets critical theory walking through a small time town in a big time country when the day has already buried itself beneath its own excuses. If I had a hypothesis it would be that Art Music sends you to sleep then wakes you up again. An unnecessary accessory casually completes the uniform.

A tremendous second fiddle comes flying through the air.consecrated

I watch the train of thought fill up with flesh and blood from inside my empty anorak such as *a broom handle can access corners of the room inaccessible to the brush* but this is not my train so I read advice from a waiting room mag on how to knock-up something quick that an infant robot still on solids could digest. Another article has a poll on whether being sensibly obsessed with dress-sense is sensory or self censorship and another one on how to dispose of the vote for a mayor or not ballot paper in the bin I tick tick-boxes then rehearse symptoms and flip to an interesting piece on how you can take steps to ensure that Robert Johnson doesn't lose his magic.

SET 37

It was an eventful translation as nothing much happened in the original we only went to Eden to buy money. The in-our-own-words version had a squall of small change and foreign notes we ran shivering into a naturist boutique and leant on doors for support before falling laughing into the next room. Everyone in the road-crew was a private empty promise with another rogue page in the road diary. Who defoliated the green man then? Who made the sea purple? I did said the translator but I was working under pressure I replaced *air* with *blood* which was understandable and not an error of the magnitude of rendering *a crown of houses on the hill* as *the sailor is home from the sea and has forgotten the language he was baptised in*. Open prison.

Customs officer violates the instrument. Open prison.

Prefect finds reproduction a chore sucking misery through a beard while the milk straw wilts towards a wandering chakra legging it to a chakra clot. Prison visitor's prefect badge gives access to a flagship full of hermits on Mondays and a prison ship full of reptilian Head Boys on Tuesdays the rest of the week he's free to draft rough reports then burn them gently to keep warm without psychological suggestion pressurising the impropriety of woodwind upon his fear of banishment to the liminal crush between city and green-belt letting 'em know he can't ride a bike even across wasteland or whistle but if he could he'd merrily blow *every death of a head of state is a small victory* then bike back biting back the governance of caked respect for a sad loner's backlogged catalogue clone loser joke pinpointing the me in he as a clown meddling with his medals. Open prison.

How exact and exacting is ethical success? Buried cash blossoms faithfully every year into sticky flowers whose poison is no longer functional. Evening, a violinist walks us to the tomb soon the sun will go down and we will go mad as the horror film begins with *a little nervous laughter*. Go through the rude door into Kate Bush's dressing room to find unfilled stocks and share options in an extreme sports company. This is the liberal world, baby, where sympathy is random. Shelley owned a timeshare in a parallel world. Open prison.ex directory

SET 38

Undiluted weeping from the in-laws in the playhouse the estuary licks the workhouse into the shape of a sappy gift-shop sandpiper improvising a cocktail from a swan's fruit pie and a corrupt copper but the sink-school teacher from Salford crying after a night of vandalism said *education gives us the knowledge to make informed choices* what she meant was it gives dignity strength and strength dignity but from here she's a broken beast the spark is gone and the pension is middle-income.ice-cream wars

You are quite charming but you are heretical. We are trench owls we don't move in any season we are tougher than a forced march and though this is the first time we've been in the First World War it's the second time we've seen the Second we watch you drag yourselves your guns and your horses starved to the size of their prehistoric dog-sized cousins up to the front. Right to the front. Right up in front of everyone. Right up there as large as life. Faces glowing.

Faith and charity against all hope. Cedilla wept for hours.

Outside the school gate mother ships chat the daddy ships are under the sea or under the hill except those who could do 365 press-ups on the surface of the sun, if they had to. Humdrum muso dreams amuse the newborn their stage-names already on Rock's waiting list. You look celestial this morning, cool and distinctly unbiological, but why are you crossing the playground as if you were treading on a grave? The piper at the gates of dawn is dying of coca cola poisoning. School gates pushed and pulled.

What a tall chap you're getting my little man. What's that you've got there? Who taught you to play that? Who taught you to play that like that? Who told you you could sing an uncontrollably straight line? What a large tree to play jazz under. What an enormous wood to play art music for. What an outsized orchestra pit to fill with lucky ears and trench foot. What a wagging tongue you have there Mr Thesaurus. The rich and their resentments make their envy of the poor too rarefied to be captured on film. The 5 to 9 social worker won't be a weekend National Trust volunteer for finishing off what they intended to start some fine day. What a flying caesura!

Set 39

They tumbled upright down the road in a rush for adrenalin though time meant nothing at the time they walked an energised walk fuelled by abandon and alcohol and no frame reproached them in the middle of the street foreshortening their perspective of a weekend in club-land into neon narcissism and near-naked shade. It was cold but they weren't cold. The pavements were crowded but they had all the room in their world reigning-in the horses of anyone's stable riding the greased grey macadam on a long illusion of legs topped with stains of colour spangle. Traffic, spare though it was and mostly black-cab, was building up before and behind. Goethe in the take-away.

There were only five figures in this gang of thirty, three women with two men wearing running shorts forming a British Bulldog chain with hands slippery with moist heat through atmosphere brutal with noise their screamed lip-synched song cut teeth on the crowd with heads lunging whiplashing back wide-eyed whites snapping the narrow sky for lucid seconds peppered with reverie as *one* to their drunken selves and witless witnesses but within hours Saturday night would fade into the bloodless Sabbath then *one* would be slaughtered and *one* would be butcher.

And so the attempt to flex unnoticed yet in common. A thousand cramps.

Cinderella loses a running shoe on the track's red clay she trips *tumbles* and sprawls across lanes in an attempt to come to terms with story telling tinder. The landmark novel's crystalline humanscape splinters into its own creation festers in the thumb of the original author as a simple do-good river in complex sin-sim-city whips the populace into film extras who up to that point were doing very well thank you without any poetry in their lives for example a bored rain-sodden market-day liquid-lunch would be relieved by a set-to at the bar the scuffle spilling into the street with rolling encephalitic heads of red cauliflower and the storyteller, opportunist extraordinaire, nipping out the back.innocent by a whisker

This is quite true the SF poetry enthusiast couldn't cope with new technology he dourly never owned a computer and said he never would he foretold his own future.

Set 40

Newly born race horse encased in a nautilus and request show disc jockey exchange soundbites at a blind summit a black-spot planned and scripted to pursue too tense a debate between two on a day when nothing accidental happens but *the* things I like are there too *such as* the distance between the arbitrary and the message in a bottle is longer than once around the world or writing a Setting at one sitting. An unlabeled map for a bird heading for the African bush is the same charted channel for a bird in different hands a record of psychological defeats rivers jammed with carcasses still gripping luggage days without beginning and meaning with no sound all convalesce in an estate agent's outer office where his secretary is an octopus using a compass.

They use the same mandatory dimensions for every coffin in every budget cremation *'cause Davy Crockett can't be dead Dad he can't he can't* I wanted to know why I felt so bad it was midday but we'd already been to the pictures and Fortuneswell was empty just for me and more experience of the pathetic fallacy waited only a few excursions off the island off. A fanciful heartthrob's serenade Oliver Twists its way into the final copy of a refugee coasting along chaos theory.geiger counter intuition

Say objects *I like* other than octopus and the subjects it pigeon-holes into its runic brown belly mouth its jelly mansion of rumps: Whiskas on mittens and Mahler's 7th an unscanned horizon and an uncanned handful of say-so beans. *Then mention must be made* trying to hide desire from the outside world in a phone call signing a petition in the street you realise how difficult it is to write and spell. Cuttlefish scales the heights of the disco floor swerves past transparent beds of spot-lit dance shuddering off parasitic pleasures in cloudy discs of the baby awake all night mentioning *things*.

Mention more *things*. More Jarvis Cocker and Boy George. Alarm in the book camp's boot corner thuds through a favourite Sahara thick Dune bought in Barnstaple and begun on the bus back. The nautilus strains salvaged time through mud mask expelled from *his* sandpaper insider organs then quarantines *her* soft exterior as nebulous cults fragment into a fog diced and displayed like fudge in a shop window. All games and imagery evolve in an involuntary blink into charmlessness and abstract strategy.

Set 41

Do you mind if I borrow another's words to build my mind with? With mind. With a mind ride a spokesperson mashed up in a mesh poking his first person's foot into the inner whirly-whoosh ear of the bike wheel balancing messy fear and a lack of balance upon an impromptu crossbar side-saddle. If the third person could borrow a third wheel they'd sprint when spoken to they'd be instinctively critical and shy of time's syllogism. One thing the second person doesn't understand is that all the people in the world today all the important movers and shakers as much Buddha bless them as the unimportant moved and shaken were at one time parallel children to *me* somewhere in the world that was—how could they have done what they did without being seen doing it in the *mind's eye* the whole thing is too bizarre to credit. OK I do believe it but only because the alternative is even harder to believe. And what is the alternative I hear you tiresomely ask I don't hear you ask it not really only the all-in-the-family melody of the computer fan and the keys' cushioned clunking that have borrowed nothing from the keyboard on which they clunk. There is nothing to give back ideally or in person. Not even wishful thinking can change the sex of the bicycle.

The paragraph above is none too clear it's about people making up their own lives by using what other people leave out of theirs and then imagining they are uniquely viral. I've a mind to put forward the proposition that we are what we are now only because nobody else sees it that way.sweet Mesmer

It's late spring a macho tree surgeon from the west midlands lobs off limbs as the wind prophesies autumn then later in the summer camp than usual the mad tree sprouts leaves as thick as the span of a top-heavy man's man not that handy but not underhandedly irrelevant either. An idle giant waited for the same summer and the strongman competitions an idol hung from his neck weighing as much as the fall of an empire it wasn't quite eternity going into reverse just a case of being idolised for making ends meet. The apprentice carpenter banging up the scenery for the latest Big Brother has a stepfather called Joseph he keeps himself to himself behind the smug medium of an inane smile at weekends he's a loinclothed rock climber tossing himself raw against a cliff made of the rules of cricket. And who are these strangers and why are they pretending they know more about me than my name could tell them?

SET 42

Uncompleted European capital cities in the early 1950s are the most complete cities. The taxidermist takes a taxi what else to the pub for his daily half-pint to ponder in parts if the current obsession with the question of nature or nurture is down to nature or nurture. He returns from the local as though it was a very long way hacking through the woods in irrational fear at first of Prussian Königsberg then in half-ration fear of communist Kaliningrad before emerging late into the sleepy light of rural England all fear ebbing into the shadows except a childhood terror of geese.

Swimmer wakes thrashing for breath through rhetorical vices gets up goes to the pool and slips in compensation. He can give up his job now and become a super consumer. I'm just going to pop over to North American cities of the 1960s and manoeuvre the hoover around a bit or to be more precise I'm going to clean-up an absolute point in space-time become a modern male a hovering-around-the-house-husband a model of replete absolution and in a stalled moment invite the world to party giving it crackers to sweep and bio-literature to coexist with sitting up in bed in the Amsterdam Hilton surrounded by flashing bulbs. When the going got tough the tough got formulaic.

I've never found the Romantics particularly romantic. The corpse of Lorca turns up in bags of mulch at an English garden centre.

They watched a cultural cameo display they made no judgements they were free.

The racehorse came flying over our garden hedge and broke its legs against the side of the house the jockey survived he now works in a laundry in a grey bacteria world. Confabulation accounts for epistolary regrouping. In a cave in the Pyrenees they found a 175,000 year old jockey ancestor a skeleton made out of silk and held together by thirteen joke balloons one burst and released a stale curse what a confab the wrong diagram of the abyss appeared in an avant-garde bible but nobody was up in arms or taken into heaven to fall balled up in nuggets of ice because nobody recognised it as an architect's drawing they thought it was your actual *abyss* but it wasn't and it isn't so nothing happens and this happens absolutely complete without set theory.well I never did

Set 43

I have a dream said Dr. Martin Luther King *I was in this yard back home and I had a chicken's head that fell off every time I turned my head and everyone was dancing and the sky was a funny colour.* I had a dream too Martin I wrote a funny poem and in it I was Peter Pan it had lines like *it's awfully windy Wendy.* The past is rubbish but it's burnished rubbish because you tried to rub it out you can't because crap goes down one tube then returns electronically through another so concentrate hold on you're getting older even old don't slip back into lending library mode or slip up on the same slimy shine that chokes the shredder. Captain Hook cackhandedly impales the leaves in the park he doesn't hold onto the job for long. On the landscaped borders of the bypass the trash sticks in the young trees. Look, a blue nightdress.

Senses dampened by routine I notice three varieties of mushroom where before there wasn't even one I develop an interest in mushrooms as an adventure develops tragedy and look them up in the Observer's Book of Merry Men to observe their photographs. After finding the three varieties a second time my less than scientific side interprets their behaviour as friendship but to no avail the original three fungi disappear like the little people back under the short cut frost.sniper's spleen

What is art about then? A re-enactment of a daring rescue? The only thing on the menu? Does *a celebrity cook discovered a continent he could call a level playing field* qualify? Art is a halfway house between utility and magic. A mob is no obstacle to art. A naked day without landmarks is perfect for a vast alien scribble but it won't botch art. Art is a rat with an idea e.g. wishing to write an insatiable poem about the different ways the young (the Lost Boys) and old (Mr. Darling) have of looking at the world. However this desire isn't in exploring the subject itself because that's a known quantity and it's not in the result because that's a known quality. Just as the mushroom is neither plant nor animal so the poem is neither embryo nor dictation or the self-discipline of a curved space. Just so I fell for the window cleaner's spiel. He called me boss so I paid him too much for imitating coordinated movements. We know what art isn't even without an assistant for the weather is the window cleaner's fickle friend and a ladder an archway of resistance to unconscious gravity pulling new muscles. What is poetry then? An answer? No, it's a sentimental horror, an unstable skill.

Set 44

Engaged to an oscillating feed. Attended by a simple disagreeable device with complicated attached advice. Fed. Attended. As in went to school. Found. As in found like that by a nurse sent by the agency. Agent as in found poem etc.

Dilate.from end to end in under 1 minute 77 seconds

To be disrespectful of someone's uncool record collection is to be unnecessarily polite to yourself. When these pages are duplicated in a Selected Chocolates the operation will be abandoned the surgeon and nurses walking off to their respective lockers leaving me alone to listen to Schoenberg's Verklärte Nacht on loop as I wait to wake or die. If the music stopped I would hear my blood following the white coated ones into swimming bath changing rooms. It takes longer to read a page by John Wilkinson than to write one of mine a nurse reads me a page as if I was in the children's ward it takes him longer to get home from the hospital than it does to do a shift. He juggles bus routes, no difference. The bus company juggle finances, no difference. At night the hospital grounds become a soul zone. We all have a lost fiancé wandering somewhere within a childlike drawing of the soul zone which is too sad as in *too cool*.

Sequence: incidental harvest.

The birth of a back street abortionist meets the requirements of GCSE English. This basic no-frills consultation is a put-up-front neo-knees-up turning a November wasp into that air ambulance that costs the health authority too much driven high above the riven peregrine falcons buzzards and herons of the woods on its round-about trip whirlwinding down river dizzily misting over specialised peasant fatigues in midst of the unknown civilian donated to the planet in lieu of their St. Christopher medal stubbornly still dangling in zero gravity capsule, or something like that. Nobody waits for psychic disintegration any more they just get on with the unwholesome business and pinch frisky happiness where and when e.g. a phenomenological wholesalers where the employer annually gets sent a grant application by some obscure outfit called *Etc. Dreams*. On the border of sleep the sound of the owls calling to each other across the allotments is a primeval creation of the here and now.

Set 45

Archival grind.

Good riddance to your amens and omens before you take this upon yourself dressed as a woman *going out* in red snow *taking out* Angela Carter for A Level as if it were a fish and chip supper consisting only of what we used to call white sauce. The factories wracked the temples ached and workhorses reduced to atomised homework suffered the golden stained insomnia. The books are made of trees after the fact.

The fairy was very pretty but her dimple was bigger than she was. She looked like a maelstrom into which we would whoosh. The woods swept around themselves then wept themselves rotten. A twisted tongue in a cynical clock wound them up.

The machine was going through an awful crash when pale 50s rock turned into sharp 60s pop. It went in as a motorbike and came out as a scooter. The scooter had another near-fatal mishap when the sharp 60s pop turned into 70s mud. It went in as a scooter and came out as a private jet and a convoy of articulated trucks. I don't just blame drugs for this because the list of culprits is endless even though it does eventually end childless.i didn't quite die on the stage but I wanted to

The skin of the magnetic lake sulks flake after flake slakes as *duende* dust floats on a swallowed surface of innuendo as if it were a flamenco in a vacuum flask. Similarly between a donated knick-knack B&B on the seafront and the actual sea there is a road gouged out scared and gorged since the late 40s by gorgeously ugly pantomime artistes who continue to crawl across the seafloor of their world like dragged anchors.

Cliché papier-mâché infant amphibians get their pilot's licence listening to the clean complex sound of the High Numbers. Young man inherited a publishing house and lived in it. He grew old in his twin brother's autobiography. Every other odd pulped feather. Regulated shock becomes patterned by the hour. A lamb fell into a ditch and the heat of noon melted its tiny memory away. Dusk, the lamb shivered awake. Night, the lamb returned to the random world with its rather too rash distortions. An A4 fleet manoeuvres in response to radar playing catch-up with an itch.

Set 46

In the 50s us kids dressed-up I got into the habit of living a literal life not a literary one they're the same thing only when there is no independence of thingy things like Desmond Morris's naked apes Morris Dancing from thingless backed orthopaedic sandals such as *man*. Unhistoricised pirates the pirates themselves insist on it only kidnap unhistorisised Indian girls the Indian girls insist on it. After childhood I was ripe for surrealism as surrealism was ripe for zoology there's something in that because *if I had my time again* I'd *like to work with animals* it's a pataphysically healthy thing for a thingy human to do with a human life span but on a long course interrupting life as war did my parents' I'd learn such figures as ponytail coarse with fatty shit and flies hoops from a girl's skull in the 50s so by the 90s business boys synchronised flicking 'em and everyone was saying *So?* Hop-scotch is democratic synaesthesia.lads gamble away their genuine moon rocks

Wanted to make a film of a house without walls where everything is as it should be including floors ceilings doors and windows but no walls you can see through to the street but having decided that I then have to consider the behaviour of those living in the house and passing it will they behave normally as if the walls are opaque or normally as if the walls are transparent? I can't even make myself up deciding. This filmmaking is not as straightforward as was first thought even when talking shop.

The forecasted language stays the same but the weathermen age tastefully winking at the weathergirls about to do their annual striptease for charity as famine sweeps Africa under the magic carpet. It's all very well for an article to laugh at hairstyles of dead decades but at the time those styles were adroit not just a foul silhouette and the boys and girls who wore them were aesthetically mortgaged. It's not change I'm against being all for every face-dancing year zero no it's the refusal of journalists to acknowledge that outside of journals people exchange scripts while slavishly fitting into stunt rolls. Who could we expect to understand this? Well, the dead, obviously. One of those dead was a kid up the road who put headlights on his go-cart he *did it up* then flashed down the 1 in 4 there were so many of us 'cause we'd boomed to rule the street our dads were immobile so we put more lights on our scooters than there were mirrors on mum's dressing table we *did them up* then flashed forward.

Set 47

The class were practising for the three-legged race in class they were a top infants' class they couldn't go in the playground because it was raining they all hoped it wouldn't be raining in two days time when sports day was to be held on the school field. Not *all* but so what. The class teacher asked her Head to help separate a pair of children who'd been practising for the three-legged he asked her in return what she was talking about did she mean that her knotted scarf was too knotty and tight or something of the sort *no* she replied *you must come and see for yourself* he did he saw what she meant the children were joined together like Siamese twins. Melded is the word. The Head was last seen kneeling on the left child as he tried to lever the right child off he was seen thus by visitors some of whom were stiff nobodies frankly but some were very important for one's professional future frankly.can-can

An adult literacy gremlin opens the literary festival with the words *let the games commence*. A brusque secret between aesthete and trainer leaks from the 4th dimension and pulses through an artificial intellect hanging off the scaffolding of a structure that is being simultaneously erected and dismantled or it could just be the illustration for a collection of short SF stories whose connection with those stories is minimal but who cares its function is purely futuristic i.e. an aid to selling but this is not that this is parole out on parole. An Animal Farm courtroom scene everyone sat on bales of hay except the accused standing in the manner of a settee balanced on its end. The judge, a right cow, says *is this picture of a gigantic snowman standing in the middle of the sea with a palm tree sticking out of one shoulder and a volcano out of the other with the title Snowman is an Island yours?*

I am named Wafer Moth. I'm not I'm only called Myra Hindley. When I was given the last sacrament twice it wasn't because I needed or earned it it was down to manhandled language. What's your name? *Fraud, my name is Fraud.* When I gave myself a poetics based on variations of a sketch in which a picket of striking fireman have to call out a Green Goddess because their fire in a barrel gets out of control then nothing could possibly be amiss but it wasn't askew enough I ask you just as there must be more to Sappho then we can see above the water so there must be less of Homer's sublime clowning below it. I can't be named Wafer Moth for nothing can I?

Set 48

The truth remains deformed by inexperience. No matter how attached involved native or alliterative our emotional switches may be the miscellaneous of the moment that Machiavellian pear-shape will override it. Arrived back at the play-station without a skeleton to my name.

I was thinking about capitalism again often do don't you? I was considering the levels of interest and emotional involvement with the nature of their product experienced though not necessarily expressed by those who work in the top echelons of a multinational company. Take McDonald's any personal interest in the actual burgers must miraculously grab touch taste before crossing the boredom threshold so any interest and involvement must be transferred to the only abstraction that counts and that's called money. It's a terrible situation so where will it lead? You can understand a politician's soldier-on sense of engaging with power-design because those golems with the rusting facades reproduce protestant ceremony in wholesome products drawn and quartered for control but the corporate touts sell tickets that are more alluring than the show itself. The small print on the rear of the modern world is calligraphed by Plantagenet loons the boredom of business a flock of mockeries circling over the deflated corpse of a swollen headed therapist.

It was a page-turner mind you, every page so awful that you quickly turned it and before you could say first-aid aid the book was finished. Consider, an alien *lands* on a land and the probability is that the apian will sink or the avian fly but that is only an alignment of probabilities. Not so with a company, friend, oh no, a company is faux-family a friend disappearing for a sec beneath organic confetti. A company leads us away from terrible things. The remains of truth are the beginnings of a rich fantasy life. Will the world be saved by its inexperience? *One can only hope for the best* while two can despair and three can give an alibi to an abetted suicide.cartwheeling through the planetarium

Severed root rotting in the fountain breeds true. Want to make the word *suburb* superb again. Every hybrid font desires that novelty.

Set 49

Get this down quickly before it gets us down beneath *an absolutely mental* average breakdown truck savagely greased up for immortal feeling the tracks will come to a sudden stop though the sleepers will pace themselves further into obscure obsidian hills. Carry On Filming must leave a mark, theoretically. Irritating adverts are the least spiteful the one where the mum tries to squeeze juice from a cranberry so her boy can be cool with the corporate cherry knowing that economies of scale are nothing to do with lexical probabilities, just repressed games. Admit it, a confessional box professional lacks a system but energy, his heraldic abstraction, is as embarrassing as an endless west country arrrrrr rolling towards land's end.nymph fatal bias tinted gas

This might not be the most pressing question for News Night but it's the one I find myself asking is there a difference or not between the quality of experience of someone who for example writes about their experience in what we call a moving and highly successful way and that of someone who writes of their experience in a poor uninspiring way? I'm not talking about literary worth itself but of the aporia between such value and the experiential reality. It could be extended to include those who do not write about their experiences except that's already implied in both options. I spent hours trying to talk about this once then the sun came up and I admitted defeat.

It was not the same day as the eclipse but it was the same cast in the same scenery.

On the bus home from town one late afternoon I saw a dog that had been run over the dog was not on the bus it had not been run down by the bus I don't know what vehicle had run it over it was laying desperate eggs of sorrow in the middle of the road. There was blood. It was wagging its tail. I should say its tail was doing that movement we call wagging because it obviously wasn't wagging in the usual sense. Apart from the wagging tail the dog was motionless on its side in the blood in the middle of the road. I think a rope trailed from its collar so maybe it was a Big Issue dog. It was black or black and white a collie-cross type medium sized mongrel. I was upset. I like dogs. Are you upset? Do you like dogs?

Set 50

There is no interval between dreams they converge picture-boards. The script for a compressed day out contained Ed Dorn singing the praises of Craig Raine we waited for motorways to *merge* or did I nod-off long before the Potteries? I might have a new friend who's into the history of psychoanalysis but the future of tailor-made dreams quits a heuristic nitty-gritty. Something gets *put in* but nothing can *come too* either as if I'd never lived or what's said out loud couldn't be worth its roots.

Fragments of an immanent prayer melting on a foreign tongue cannot be done over.

Aged seven I used to go on holiday every two years to my Nan in Ireland and between the biennial realities I used to dream of going on the journey and sometimes arriving but quite often not quite both before and after the journey itself. The cathedral drips up into the heavy August sky and mustard yachts race from trick Napoleonic tricolour to tricolour across the harbour. Ruined castles surround every aspect of the water—a limerick competition is in full swing.the ocean we belong to is a dissolved marriage

Lamp lit fugue fruit. Red White and Blue looks Green White and Orange through Lucozade yellow every colour displaced by over-done heaven with no gap between nuns their continuous block of solid black topped with windburn cheeks and white-bandaged foreheads beneath which a witch migraine twitches. Dock at dawn by mid morning after customs queuing we're walking the streets of the town knee deep in golden shit fallen from green horses and orange cows. Horse-drawn carriages carry us over the streets of gold excrement while yet sticking in the smell. Beguile a while. The regatta is in a rush to finish. An Irish Rousseau didn't paint this he built it. An Irish Blake didn't write this he smelt it. I am not a tourist I was buried here as a baby I belong here in a way that Drake and any other criminal English dickhead doesn't.

This song is about Elton John but not sung by him it's one of the few treasures I've ever succeeded in bringing back from the isle of darkness: *This man is dy dy in' / this man is dy dy in' / this man is dy dy in' in young man's grass / young man's grass / this man is dying in young man's grass.* Send a blank tape and I'll send you the tune.

SET 51

Occasional spelling the odd spell right here and there scattering the I Ching in temper as in scattered jigsaw when a fractured picture-cow is supposed to throw-up a nursery rhyme or does the rhyme dice the cow up as the moon is a spoonful of sun. I couldn't spell or jigsaw I lacked patience and skill and if visual discrimination was lacking along with a suitably sharp word-saw who couldn't be bothered to kick and cry god damn it jESUS this is not about you it's about me and my mild mannered voodoo hand-me-down daytime phantom friend in the room of the amnesiac.

In feely-box city in the guise of a mock-naive painter Adrian Mitchell announced my poem was joint second as the frigates leaving for the sun saluted an embarrassing pun passing Devil's Point. A friend took her dog there for a limping lunch-hour walk once she picked up a lame marine uniform to marry he wasn't an Adonis he was from Sunderland that's an echo of Pete Brown meeting Venus on the cliffs of Bristol years later the dog's legs were shaped like hockey sticks but even more years later I took Andrew Duncan for a walk there he talked about local government and we disturbed some fishermen as we dropped names into the harbour *mop mop courgette* curvy corvette both fat and svelte quoth both didn't know any better than to put this in a letter so I chucked it together and I chuckled as I did it and my tongue bled when I bit it *oh I do like to be beside the sea whose side can only bleed water.*added extract

An anonymous reef. A seething apocalyptic playground.

Reading his old diary in an old dairy Rimbaud got a day off school because of a dose of narcolepsy he reminds me that on my first day at school a little lad with hair blonder than I ever experienced before Heinz and Jet Harris called me names that before that moment weren't mine he called me a *slow-coach* we were actually sat in a gold and lacquer black stately coach that though stationary flew from the convent into a future pulled by hearse horses. His little legs dangled over the edge of the cushioned seat but mine were sticking out of the side of my head. I felt as if I had always existed but only this nasty boy knew it. Well, was I a slow coach or not and what did it mean and why was it said in the frozen simulacrum of the inside of a carriage when it had no exterior shape to belong in? Still trying to learn the lesson of that day.

SET 52

In *space books* they have a saying about saving space as you would save oxygen silly science fiction and all that early rock-n-roll my dad is young he kicks the air through the space between the radio and the kitchen door and the pre-booked empires become no more than an avenue of venues. It's not the season for sludge but sludge fills the busy quantum void between good reads and bad readers. I say I say. Turn up the volume. I'm sure I know that language they're singing in in the space opera.

Miming puns make forms of singular interest like little muffins with chocolate-ice hats stamped with tiny symbols of dollar swag. In real life I've probably been up top on an open-top double-decker bus about four times but in dreams it must be closer to forty but no more a conductor on his busman's holiday in a paisley blue-striped shirt who disagreed with my politics advanced down the aisle then stabbed me.

There is a field of wind. A field of sand. A field of paper.relief light

Geese open their parachutes and eat their lunch. Goose at a motorway station gets up on the weighing machine that tells him to *ger off*. The ghost of a silk grey parachute billows behind the swollen carnivalesque head of an assassin hiding in the hot fur costume as the basketball team's mascot fox. Shine the torch though the torch is dim shine the torch on the scene between rocks wet with urine though the torch is dim shine the torch on the embrasure where the peripherals of death don't bother to listen in lessons. The scene is covered in pirates' t-shirts khaki shorts and baseball boots abandoned there since the war between the Braden Gang around (not over) the hill and our afternoon alliance of playing groups (not play groups) just about little and tough enough to gang-up. In the days before Polaroid when I managed a sub post-office with Monopoly notes and owned a fleet of windjammers romantically a long time ago in sun cycles and bramble moon spans. Underwaterwear left under bushes was never plural. Heaney's blackberries just don't work for me and it's down to that.

Tramp sleeping on ramp in empty reservoir woken by Roman war-machinery. Siege-mentalitied by Alice-like logic he bursts into tears and the reservoir fills like a blow-up doll. Mark Wallinger's horses work for me but Muldoon's don't.

SET 53

She said *the heron is very clever. What* he said. *The heron is very clever* she said *it can dive for its supper and sit high in the tree with a view of me and you. Clever* he asked *why is it clever? Because it can dive for its supper and sit high in the fir tree looking around and digesting its supper* she replied. *Clever eh* he said *but it hasn't got Sky. Yes it's got Sky* she replied. *It's got Sky then* he replied. *Yes it's got Sky. Has it got cable* he asked? *Yes it's very clever it's got cable. It's clever and it's got cable? Yes, and Sky.*

I tried to write a mainstream poem but I couldn't I put *he slouched his long young bones against the perspex of the bus-stop* in order to contrast him with the old lady standing painfully upright in the bus-shelter on her short old bones. I thought the contrast between them would give the poem its backbone but it didn't do anything it just waited for the next bus. His eyes didn't register hers and hers didn't register his but their registers were different blanks. I thought through the day that through the day at bus-stops such as this such young men must always be happening around the same time as such old ladies because town beckons both when they no longer have to answer to their different registers.you can't cheat a fairy tale

A drawing of Saturn done in red and black biro by my granddad Jim still bookmarks the musty calculations foretelling the date when Thomas Hardy and his Magic Show gets double-booked with his Punch & Judy Show. Lacking logic but not a good pair of leather elbow patches we pub-crawl past the mermaids in their crystal-ware underwear while watching over our shoulder patches (every now and again) for when the grey shadow of a lumpen moon scatters the future behind us in scrunched-up silverfoil. Every now. Every again. And when the congregation of now and agains constitute a riot of artificial life Tess rises from the mattery grave to smile for Man Ray's lens but the man isn't there *no more* he's gone the way of the bleached-out grail but the Kodak goes clickity click on its clever lonesome saying *yes yes that's it* as the Tess corpse *makes love to the camera.* The entire cast catch the bug.

Excel at what you do. Gems are eventually crushed by the weight of spider webs but chewing gum and its descendants become the dominant species. Sell what you do.

Set 54

Re-expression of value e.g. a novel about seedy street life uses seedy street life as instrumental scene while seedy street life in a poem is a birthday treat from Altered Images. The differences between literary fiction and poetry are under-determined.

A light communism never tired without climaxing, never tried. Soundproofing the studio with stale bread. Common mystery, honey-brushed with paranoia and promise. Mirror thickening. Mirror streaked with image seepage. Fair-mindedness runs for office or is that just run to the office dropping the curriculum vitae somewhere between toothpaste and the tube. Spinning scarecrow CDs re-expressed light's numb obsession as heavy spade work bent the silhouettes on the allotment today but now past midnight looking for my lost dog there is nobody in the collapsed distances except fluttering darkness and the shadows of shadows. Heart clad in fungus.

The brazen of tanked-up lads had no tanks but it didn't stop them cruising Plymouth shouting *Let's get some Saddams*. This is a beautiful country and I shall return to it one day as I am now returning to my subject but this is not an anti-war poem it's not enlisting in any anthology because if Blair-Bush was here and I had a gun I'm sure I would fire it not one hundred percent sure mind my pacifist spite could just result in spit or even a silly smile. If anything this setting is pro-war a celebration of being British a song for the tough pale squaddie who can bend his bullets as the local rag said *like Beckham's free kicks and slam into the raghead's chest killing him instantly* it's a reassuring reminder that the event can be relayed back with such clean detail it's the healthily warm expectation of the Brit sniper getting a medal pinned on his chest because the Iraqi's chest was splattered through by his free kick it's a respectful celebration of that and a new song we should be proud of such things and thank the necessity for them thank the powers that be for giving us the opportunity of acting that way and talking that way and letting the world know that we can learn a lot from the Americans about irony as contrary to popular myth they're even more ironic than us oh yes. A lousy astronaut and a great astronaut exchange stories and can enjoy their respective tales not so much as sober information in drunken subtitles as shrunken objectives amidst gross cigar shaped objects.inflated scar tissue

Set 55

Come through thread even in pokey threes we call 'em Flintstone trees we can handle it the patterns of pretty stitches with dainty eyes holding ribbed recall to a 60s sitcom which if called correctly answers to the name Compact a women's magazine in half-hour concentrate of office adventure drawn to an alignment of fem-commerce and the common cold but in cluttered handbag memory it's Harpers set in a city department store with John Leyton singing Johnny Remember Me. Joe Meek made that record made the world seem simultaneously romantically young and ghostly the maids in the class turned dreamy and so did I weak in the knees with poetic power promotion. All was fantasy except the power it was postmodern charm 1961 an actor pretending to be a pop star by making a real record but the hired Rhinemaidens invading the store for his promo reached out with truly lovesick eyes their casual hands coquettishly brushed his sleeve then dipped into him as if he was the Rhine. The NT reconstruct an NUT conference from the late 70s.fashion as birthright leftism as thrifty

The headlines are particularly long this evening: *Don't Care was made to care Don't Care was tried Don't Care was hung 'til he died then he didn't care so where's the jousting in that?* From the newsstand a painted by numbers Michael Douglas barks theatrically *Plasma trace of the prodigal* as his misses falls straight from Hello onto the caked filth floor of the booth's hellish inner recesses. The clever observer will connect this with clever Laurie Lee and Robert Graves as Penrose sculptures appear in the House of Lords' lobby and on classroom shelves but the connection with Lee Miller following the G.I.s into the camp with her camera to finally connect with a never not topical old Europe is as yet only an infinity of sixth senses expressed as a government utility as if mannerly saluting fascist in the shower to rinse underarm could ever be acted out without thinking it a harmless game of consequences.

When there is little to talk about talk about the person who cannot stop talking. Still trying to think of a name for *our group* still trying to *make something up*. All through the summer in the streets of the town and the lanes of the countryside the AA and the RAC fought their territorial war ambushing the story before it too became too true in fictional media. Paragraphs implode like space litter. When one earring swings free the other is a hermit crab.

Set 56

There is no time left but there is so much light left that even 1970s small press poetry is readable. Father-in-law hypnotises himself by asking how those vast ferry chains can even be made let alone linked I say *I saw a programme about it once*, but I never, I'm just making light of time hanging heavy. If I smoked I'd be chain smoking, but I don't. Double glazing sales advert actor tells us the sound of the lad learning to play trumpet is painful but can be muffled by two panes though he's not that direct it could be wrong and *in life* the sound of the wind coming through a window's aperture is a muted trumpet so under scrutiny negatives never quite match their positives a lesson taught by both poetry and advertising. Cute kid know-how is a trope's pre-destiny e.g. it's no good understanding the way a metaphor such as *laying your cards on the table* influences life post-poker without witnessing it emerge pre-game. But let's assume as much as we can. The politics of the performing cheats on the charity record is private yet a privateer never saw himself as irrelevant. Scrutinising for any luck lying around on Millbrook's foreshore I picked up a salt soaked sinister inscrutable cat carving thinking *a ship's cat emigrating from Egypt to Sol.*t talking b bout T Townshend Ave.

Forefathers in the old country emigrated to the US to create Cardinal Spelman and Spiro Agnew and I'm proud to be a rusting lyre half submerged in a fake lake.

Possible Fast Show sketch? A woman is walking along a high street struggling with bags of shopping. A car approaches slows down and hoots and the woman looks up and recognises the driver who waves. She smiles broadly and tries to wave back but can't because of the bags however in the attempt to wave she drops a bag then manages to give a quick little hi with her hand but while struggling to continue its suggestion of a wave the other bags slip and the assorted groceries spill onto the pavement and roll into the road. She can wave freely now, but she doesn't, her arms hang limp and she smiles mutely at the back of the car carrying on down the road. We watch it disappear. Cut. This scenario is repeated in various versions throughout the series and gets funnier every time until a point is reached where it is no longer funny but extremely comforting. The series ends and we miss it. When I first read this Set to my fan club they thought it was an actual Fast Show sketch I could tell and my breathing became incoherent. A dilettante reflects.

Set 57

While deep in the shallows of a dry dream is there a walking-on-water word for the lost and forgotten apart from lost and forgotten synonyms? Did Foucault have such a word out of a hat? *Who won the raffle?* asks Foucault he really wants to know. Who history cannot be both what is remembered and what is not if there's a hysterectomy of the *word* apart from history and its antonyms and in the engorged question, what colours and preservatives? *You bet* said Alan when Allen asked if literature was important then Allen knew it was even less important than ever but Alan thought it was even more important still. The way Rimbaud pronounces *Allen* has extraordinary significance for academia nuts. The judge and accused are tongue-tied but they can both see through the jury to shop-soiled anonymity. Never been beach combing but I've combed the beach many times says a lot like a Which Magazine witch trial.

Hinge and Bracket get the connective juices flowing. Selective loss.

Until the 13th of always I'll still be a vibrating funny bone. Lack-lustre baby stuff like two turds having a bath in the sink. My redheaded mum made the washing very white then we exercised singing green rebel songs. Fingers were hinged chips. Greasy orange fungus oiled the dolphin for his cross-channel booze cruise. The sillier and more inconsequential the game the more Jesus cheated which must say something from the slave trade to Smash Hits the established rave in their certainty and the disestablished go to their own empty church I'm not saying that as a criticism cHRIST it's not even an observation it's a mirror made of bricks. Has anyone got a collected Creeley I want one as close as possible to this side of his *so long* when the collected has to be amended before all second-guesses roughly date this's original.see-saw

It's a very important meeting but it's slowing down. This evening we have a very important meeting and as it approaches I'm mutating. This is public stuff made personal tonight we have a very important meeting but it is already over it's all over the news they say travels fast. A favourite piece of cinema in German Danish or Swedish or something a film purposely grainy amateur and shaky about a collective pretending to be retarded and they visit an adventure park I really liked that it was as if they were kids at Woodlands or Crealy Adventure Park. Off-ground chase.

SET 58

If the door is open and the door is wide enough the fly that flies in will be the fly that flies out. But look at the face of the fly that flies in, Bertrand Russell? Now look at the face of the fly that flies out, heaven knows who it is but it isn't Russell. The wreck in the bay was beautiful on a beautiful day means that logically Bertrand Russell is still in the room. It is cooler in the room and more beautiful than an ungainly aesthetic theory but a composite of all our commercial rivals is the heartfelt tug of a *singing from the same hymn sheet* rival restaurant's Herring Trifle. The artist pouts as he draws fishing boats. This is a conventional prose poem then then along comes the notion that life is a block of frozen cherries. If the particularity of the metaphor isn't itself what determines its quality then it doesn't really matter where you, as an individual, are positioned within the block of cherries because that has no bearing on its being a block of cherries, or not e.g. being positioned a moment before death or the moment you first read about The Smiths in the Daily Mirror or the moment you first thought of this frozen block of cherries or the moment when you were at your coldest at Whiteworks in the middle of Dartmoor in the middle of winter and it was so cold you'd have died had you not been running around like a mad thing or the moment after you were born when you had no notions melts in the mouth like any other language. Anyway, if you have no notions then you are not positioned in the block so the whole articulated arctic edifice melts it's good job I didn't take too long or put too much effort into this cherry picked biographeme.sophist trigger figure

Artificial contexts for saying things. The clever dick was explaining the difference between literature and volleyball by using a poem about volleyball as an example: *Everything said must be given a context or have its usual context taken away.* What's that got to do with volleyball? *Exactly.* Intelligent Richard implied everything must look contextual, boltholed to be there, at home like a swan in a swannery, and that's the art. What for? *For the sake of anything which is not beach cricket but beached cricket or beached volleyball for that matter or even beached poetry picnic with burning logs twilight bad guitar bad wine bad poems and good friends.* Young work colleague of my mother dived hit a rock and spent the rest of his natural in a wheel chair. He went back to work and became cranky instead of civil in his service yet I've laughed more in my life than cried so that must be saying something else.

SET 59

Genuflect in an irrigation ditch to supernatural creditors tax-free on the red planet driving too fast to be recognised or to recognise anyone going too slow to be noticed as a better life somewhere once a distant colony that got dangerously close.

Carefully reappearing at the correct time and place.printer's apprentice

Sneaky elocution lesson afflicts Saturday a matinee that doesn't end until evening chill shivers and shakes you awake to the Rock 'n Roll of more dogs playing piano than there are pianos in the neighbourhood though that doesn't mean they learnt how to play the damn things properly. Similarly the provinces refuse to forgive an error made about them in the capital. These counties are actual people, all fitted up with pipe-hopes. Their citations, translated from a future language, are apprehended then misapprehended e.g. a neglected family take the blame for their neglected child. An alternative life would require different fragments but the same order. It's not a Quaker who mows the Quaker graveyard how's that for meaning sport?

My parents recognise me but haven't a clue as to what I do their dog has a clearer idea even though they haven't had one since I left home. In correct order first Boot went into the vets and never came out then I skedaddled to eat plates and plates of London peas then Mum sneaked back to gOD leaving Dad alone to dance with whomever. What I do doesn't fit any of the usual but blowed if I'm gona whine about it I'm not Tony Harrison. Brenda found the previous owner's baptismal certificate in the attic and this made me think of us in the house for twenty-one years as electricity's peaceful brute.

Identity is long and thin but has no width at all. It has repetition without return. We kinder used to play ring games in the garten but it was an Euclidian line that lead back to those terraced lawns baked first communion dresses and trespassing path going past abandoned green houses and the chemical roots of delinquency. A dream is a memory given a new tradition just as memory is a dream without a membership card. The sky is the colour of thin cucumber and it takes on other attributes of the cucumber too.

Set 60

Contrasting trees compare weathers. The idea of experiencing shade when the sun *goes right in the water* is at one remove from accumulating portentous artworks. Unimaginable guilt at what we're excluding from a multiple viewpoint trickles a cutting through the status quo. Hopkins' dappled dark souls of the night didn't help attempts to get a grade A because their madcap distraction was too mysterious to concentrate on for long before tackling the most mundane question. So this was how adults played—it was a new world but without natural landing sites or even ways of entering public conveniences without breaking some long-winded law. The seasons collaborate however threatening the exam but when a student has to engage with Hughes saying the landscape in the storm is a stretched canvas in that storm what are we to make of ourselves as non-poets, let alone people who may or may not go camping? It means you can only teach Farmer Ted with a cold breeze finding the small of your back nervous of the untrustworthy gaps in bushes from which a cartoon philosopher could pounce pin you to the sudden ground so suddenly damp then inseminate you with long incubated soul-seed for the sole purpose of coming back later to steal your soul. So that's what really happens in up-dated Eden, better move out to where prosthetic spectacles manoeuvre freely between brittle cloud.

The Settings are produced on the screen for the page so when I perform them I'm all too aware of their over-rehearsed relaxing resistance the imbalances nudged a bit but the pop-art target retreating further into the ever-decreasing centre is a bulls-eye as experienced by a shortsighted outlaw of the woods. It isn't what the audience expect first they cheer the Sheriff's champion then they cheer the masked intruder who kills him. Entertainment is at one remove from oppression as distraction is at one remove from (underline one only) torture, boredom, chaos, revenge. It was on the thousandth day of the Stanislaw Lem convention that the professional improvisers finally forgot how to kill a thousand birds with one stone. Reactionary syntax.like I said

Today being short depresses me but consider the spelling bees.

Convoluted longhand for saying that literature will not live on.

Set 61

Dark blue storm's light blue promise shapes-up let's call the pup Neutron. Neutron Neutron come here you're not as high as the handles on a horse. Heavies come to walk him by day the do-it-yourselfers later and at night two or three wobbly criminals - follow the glowing fag tips and fear for the innocence of property. Nigh impossible for mites to live peacefully in a harmonica same for studs and students in early 70s teacher training they got the oracle all wrong buried behind chalk yellow bananas and flesh pink tuck-shop shrimps 'cause the Red Army retreated are retreating still across the steppes the frozen swamps the Mongolian dunes to the sea back beneath the waves to the black world of Tanguy the blind fish and the prayers of Richard Dawkins.

The muscles in the bodybuilding magazine could so easily be torn in there. Baby birds check-in to too many hotels. Every balloon has a thought inside it nobody knows those thoughts we watch the balloons disappear into azure this is only a guess but could one thought be *shares in a plough factory are jealous of the hare's waste of space*. Stop, what just fell off the back of the wagon like bad tempered decorating? The relationship between forecaster and the weather is like that between responsible teacher and irresponsible pupil. School uniforms whether loyal to school or pupil still fade teaching nothing. On the bloated soul-bus the reserved seating is empty no standing room either even for poor Georgie Best he can't do his boots up the laces are strings of liquorish the last thing he sees before final black-out is a gang of Billy-the-Kids thirsting to see who can be first to draw a toy gun without moving parts.

Two child actors are given the job of being boy and girl rucksacks they have to act as if they are deep packs heavy with hiking gear being hauled up and down rainy fells. Somewhere in the bottom of one of the packs is a pack of Happy Families in which the Holy Family ride into Derby on a donkey. So far so good. It's a love story where parents just can't get to the bottom of either backpack so they hold a new national anthem competition and get mannequins to chase up the contestants in an alternative Commonwealth Games where the physically ill and the mentally ill battle it out in a sack while under the ruck an unsporting sensation with matching accessories gives birth to a bridge between a real word and a reel of film.tetchy alien boredom

Set 62

If every direction had purpose you could choose then a generation of palindromes.

Original sin changed to go out on the town only to see a glass blower kicked into the gutter by those who don't see through what they do so don't really mean it therefore it is almost clichéd to say there is more art in misunderstanding than in understanding so *there there* there are things almost possible but don't count on them it'd be counting trees in the hope of finding the original. The begging bear groans behind the type-cast bear's growl but only in principle does this bear despair stop when each natural-born star is the précis of a sun and I'm not satisfied that that's proof. A possible disproof educates an impossible sin. Lame snake intelligence grows more out of focus in focus group refusing to give enough credit to surf for the eventual credulity of the westcoast surf sound. The scientist said he needed a ghostwriter who knew nothing of science but would even a children's hour engine driver peckish before arriving at Paddington dive into an engine's knot of crosses for nought but his stencilled egg sandwich?

When on the ladder the window cleaner likes riddles when off the ladder he likes fishing. Little globes of the past stick on me like air bubbles on a water plant that's a simile a simile is a young metaphor that's a metaphor a metaphor is like a grown-up simile that's a simile. The dancers had taken drugs their insights were moderate yet frequent and the music had actualised size not bite-sized social realities coaxing them into the mud bath where, these days, The Group meet for what they imagine are the mental equivalent of press-ups. Friendly fire frames the fellow traveller that fellow Freud camouflaged as spiced pears that's good history is gaining new confidence evidenced in the latest street names: Malcolm Morley Muse, Howard Hodgkin Houses, Gilbert and George Terrace, Rachel Whiteread Rd., etc you get the picture you can finish off these streets yourself feel free to skimp on materials.

The Merseybeats' Suspicion blared from the always-surprised eyes of the girl in the mathematical instruments factory while staring I blundered into abstraction. The corpse of a theorist lies in the gutter but the theory flows free through colloquial silence.an animal asked a hermit

SET 63

Filthy smoke defaced fate. Moneybox sofa hid fat-cat hamsters. The hunter as writer another clichéd myth turns inside-out to be as true as the rubber tree is so far. The chartered pilot wanted to be the leading character he walked like nobody's business out of the Italian jungle with his Russian passport about to be pushed out of his shorts pocket by the correct grammar of an erection turned into an avenue of embassies and sauntered by without taking his pick. Public swimming-pool currency jingled in the other pocket. There were pockets in the face too.

A whispered stream of adjectives describes the stream. Stream overtakes the written word. A condom machine in the toilets dispenses Juicy Fruit. I think I am dreaming precognitively of a cigarette packet called Diplomat but naked and alone writing a postcard in a laundromat.obscenely optimistic

Getting sunburnt in the late 50s was an annual occurrence that went on for years we didn't understand much in those days. Cooling calamine was a closure of a summer day plus an alliterative cough cluster of Newtonian narratives tied like pies around random time gellings unveiling that model of the formation of the new town galaxies when space was *younger than that now*. Major philosophers used alternative names for the seasons because the major philosophies had found a match with a vagabond's inhibition in a hollow authenticity forced to experience the individual observer's otherwise untroubled boots by another bystander left there by a careless god. All things being equal you will notice this gasman and if they're not then at least register his white van parked outside the studio where a demonic jury of wankers are debating literary prizes and deferring to lofty reputation. I love those cup-a-soup adverts you know the ones. Angels take hyenas for their constitutional in the evening park or is it just a fashion-shoot I say *just* I mean *wow this is the kind of thing we come to London expecting* when working undercover for the Esperanto society Gomorrah is behind us but Sodom is just around the corner I say *just* I mean *wow this is* just *the kind of thing we come to London expecting.*

In Private Spirit St. stinging nettles behave like figurative speech. A sloshing index.

Set 64

We are divided only by our dreams we are united only by our star-gazing or don't believe the orange monks are doing acrobatics in the courtyard 'cause they aren't kids the same people get all righteous at the dropping of a vowel. The eldest monk unnaturally performing somersaults most vigorously is their natural impractical reader as well as their practical leader even though they swear they have no reader or leader they swear this blind they blaspheme this in public but everyone in the street uses clairvoyance to interpret this school of void-jumpers' use of more four-lettered words than the civvies but the drive of this story is really the old monk master is famous for his hamstrung sayings but it is against the rule of the order to write them down and now the sage has Alzheimer's so when the initiates repeat his sayings wrongly and in the wrong order to boot he doesn't know so he doesn't not go much on it let alone say so so it is only a light-headed sentimental sadness there for us to imagine.

Information carried by campanology fossilised nerves irritating the hell out of an anchored occult mustering of thugs armed only with sharp grass and Venus fly-trap. When burning books the librarian has a dangerous and glamorous job fear of your homeland is translated into a trivia harness. We are all based on autochthonous tease.heraldic pants be hanged

The Settings are authors of total freedom. A zoo as empty as distant laughter describes a tramp scribbling in a notebook. The pages bell, true-to-life. The longer the tramp looks at me the more he appears to recognise himself. Crap supermarket fruit warps towards why we want our literature unblemished. A third nasal passage as an anthem for the Lord is the lost results of memory glissando. At the lights a car pulls up with stereo blaring a bass-crazed garage rhythm as my fingers are already relaxed out the open driver's window against the glistening metallic blue of the car door they thrum the beat the lights change the car moves off the hand to which my fingers belong hesitates the beat. Out of sequence Gingerbread Man survives.

Paul Celan wasn't a very good Samaritan when the phone went it was always millennia before he picked it up but in the end he got the hang of it and every poor soul who rang hoped against hope that it would be Paul who answered.

Set 65

The adventure shifts in its seat. Yet another poet is *the most exciting and important writing in the country today* even my dog doesn't drop as many blurbing sticks at my feet as this. Contrary to modern theory I think language is stonily extraneous to reality bugger it recalling too late a blanket question required for every Set does a radiator feel its own heat it was an easy thing to forget the night is long though those who ply the darkness are quick witted. A community's mixed feelings about its joy-riders.

The view of the world given by the popular travel programme appealed to my sense of melting abundance. Once I said to Steve *I think capitalism would be fine if the price paid for it was shared out equally there is nothing inherently wrong in invisibly bright commerce* he didn't know whether to agree we found ourselves talking about John Ashbery. Like other lads and lassies brought up by the sea I require a thesaurus that never ends when trying to describe my feelings towards it *power* in my Chambers begins with *ability* and ends with *weight* and right in the middle it says *intensity, juice* but the amusing dissatisfaction functions pre-structure. A patented praying shape as patiently still as a prayer rock gently sways then definitely dances then heaves violently vomiting an immersion heater onto the shore. Down inside the sea wall there is a belt buckle unless it has completely rusted away.ununionised laundry

Mao's Long March to Glastonbury 1949 a row of toilet cubicles receive a motley of anonymous festival goers but issuing from them minutes later are an assortment of *word-people* such as Hamlet and Tom Jones whom we have to differentiate from the real Tom Jones who came later. Never knew which Tom to follow they disappeared into the crowd I hopped back to my tent a kid Long John Silver or an escapee from the Japs who took my leg off below the knee leaving me with a best friend to lean on before he left me in the parched jungle grass to scream myself towards death while he went home for his tea.

Tongue-tied folk-art screen saver depicting a narrow boat halfway across the widest part of the widest ocean slots into place piece by puzzling piece. An expedition to find the TV remote departs before curfew.

SET 66

Badgers spit out their words they don't need them a belt of newsprint reforms first edition's frost. Nobody here diets quietly the train chases deer but when it's passed the deer chase it back for exactly 5 seconds. The sky frosted flag. A pond of cognac. The magnetic virgin mother up against the fridge door says the gondolier being serenaded by his iPod spoilt her gondola ride cliché. Zen cadets learn to trace a hearsay edge of Slashy Dot. Finger-shopping internal investigator ramraided a fad bag drum-set quarrel lid and an ornamental psychiatrist off-by-heart while his clients helped to tarmac the road with the labour of their phantom limbs. Smog of techniques.

Overheard educational welfare officer what he said a size too small. On my way up Holloway Rd. to another funeral with a copy of a shark walking nonchalantly upright onto the Arc in the presence of copybook plankton reversing up the plank. All my friends became police cadets or wasted freaks. Pavement artist Huckleberry Fin chalks a breast pocket upon a stranger then a hydrant and sidewalk on an American visitor which is why I am not a poet though I have always felt like one.horse butcher

Permeable border guard gave up smoking to the roar of the waterfall stood to the rear of its smoky green glass looking at the world refracted into something beautiful—Bergson's flowing ache. David and *me* we admired Bergson's boots in the photo in the stolen encyclopaedia of philosophy we were nostalgic for the world of our great grandfathers flushed through modern rebellion.

Objects take place. Auction-room holds a harbour a city-square a blond yoghurt a box of miscellaneous collective nouns a pride of unicorns and an outrageously subtle sonnet. If there were no animals would I refer more to plants would haemophiliac flowers and tree ligatures crop up skirmish echoecho phosphorescent atrophy? The speed of thought blanking equals the speed of thought becoming while we're stalking zeros indifference floats by, sacredly. Fold up the safe bet. Fold your arms. Don't touch anything just wait. Ken Edwards waves from the window of a bus. A museum of poetry magazines takes pride of place in a fresh new city. Statement question quote: what other exhaustions are there? pPathology of shSHelves & stSTaircases.

SET 67

When they *are* presently pleasantly awake in the sun the striking miners dreamt then of victory but when they *were* asleep in the shade they'*ll* dream of damp Bach. You don't know what they are but the child who draws them knows already whether they are sails or mountains. Tomorrow born careworn *tense*. Neutral character actor plotted suicide. Stinging sting gazumps blackberry club trumps. I had to apologise *for* the baby Melanie with the hole in her heart Dad built her parents' house for nothing on Sundays. Technicians walking around the edge of the shop-floor in brown coats over their suits they might have passed their exams but Mum's ambition will make this asymmetric hippy dwarf a shifty young teacher. Another character drops in on his girlfriend's parents on his way to dropping out they chat they chaperone pedantic little truths past distant galaxies of deception. Time is a peeping tom.

It is only a full address book because so many puppets have their own addresses. And the pungent smells of overripe life in the park after a weekend of dry heat assail the senses but fail to emote by remote. It was a heavy weekend carried like a pregnancy. The future may be a fossilized cascade *yet*. Rabbits progress day by day towards the capital with their socialism in shadow and a microphone without juice but I turned-back half way and turned my kilt inside out a coward a traitor a beast but never a drunken bully in uniform or sign language. I've written so many stupid things about so much stupidity that not even honesty can be trusted.auteur valve

The battlefields of Britain from every car window and look at how many there are they outnumber our cities. The Chapman brothers should stick life-sized figurines of traffic cops without their cars on all the sites the project could be called Babblefield. A glider made of all the sauce that ever dripped down the *bottle* could take this in even if the critics remain as baffled as unpoliticised widows. None of 'em can *essay* but they know their cocktails. It's not a question of how much the IRA achieved by maiming it's about how much they prevented the Special Branch from cloning its homunculus the day always comes when the pearly king and queen are not true cockneys. The idea of employers having to make an appointment to be accepted by an employee is a sexy idea even in the Co-op. The symbol was touched. It wept solidly.

SET 68

Feeling delicate on my birthday a horizon trying to exist without a line a sacrifice without worshippers an infinity without any conception of a cul-de-sac Casualty fatality without an argument an interrogator trying to keep up with the speaking wounds wishing he'd learnt nightschool short-hand instead of chatting-up a tumour that just happened to look like a girl in the bus depot then having to confide/confront her brother/ boyfriend in the form of a bus timetable so long and complex that when vandals tried to mark/mock it they failed at even something else.

Substituted cosmos. Drawings of unsupervised cosmic occurrences. The original cosmos with its ubiquitous antique fleas and immanent blush. Strange drawing of Mr and Mrs Ordinary looking a bit jumpy because Mr and Mrs Strange are behaving normally. Scab bowling pins publicly humiliate your day in court turns to nightmare. Pastel drawings of an insolvent octopus spread across a billiard table. The table borrowed from The University of Unique Sincerity.

At rehearsals the director directed the jury *there is no such thing as free verse the future is a cell for memory to mix up some savage colours* e.g. in St. Trinians who are the servants serving could it be the bootlegged parataxis of a frozen argument sliding across leather like a polygraph? The school motto was meant to evoke the distressed eggs of a chaste mother in order to tart-up unconscious revolt but instead it punctured the skull in an attempt to restore virginity, which was plain stupid. No cosmos is irresistible. No comic is that good even when chased into puns so simple that those who spin them are unassuming hamlets.

Aerobic despair bunches treacherously yet a sleek silver train crosses a beautiful estuary on a lovely summer evening matter-of-factly crossing Zig Zag Wanderer with maze clatter passing out of the picture onto a platform of stratified gravy trained to imperceptibly camber by a gravity drain. *Rapido* slips from the travel compendium.forged titles

Folk singer's alter ego fat chat-show host interviews empty water closet.

SET 69

Too much time spent redefining authenticity is a judgement-based cold-meats counter. Blinking indefinitely is a symptom of pastry in the eye of higher vision brought down a division to the seabed when *Tender to Genre* sank without Tracey. The search party are all alcoholic Celts of one stamp or another they have their own way of getting to and through Art College without having to sign a canvas or decipher the stitched scrawl on a tent. Habit is not ritual it doesn't speak volumes it administers to a single durable space, like a mag a mug or a man. Just how wide capitalism's shoulders get within that single breasted universal lawsuit without bursting and haling the helicopter is poetic as opposed to pure speculation. Call it flattened speculation too. Where were we?eidetic blank cheque

If size doesn't matter then the bigger the dialectic discrepancy the better the rule resistance of morally bankrupt internal design. A concrete example can be made of anything, even pixels. A deformed ethnic instrument plays a variety of unsympathetic magic tunes or music limps out of the shop's black shadow into the grey shadow of the street so we go in. The shop is Colourless Narrow Narcissist Border but the couple squabbling over the purchase of an unnecessary belt accessory are modern and immune.

Claustrophobia and breathless panic conceptually flood the National Express coach. Might as well have been a slug burning in salt and that does not describe what I want it to describe it describes something else. Discomfort so gross goes through multiple-choice personalities like a flipbook and that does not describe what I want it describes something else. Referendum: which style of heat in the repetitious foreign kingdom of the poem in which I tried to describe cliché socially but ended up on all fours in the ventilation shaft scraping the air from its floor with my tongue - a liberal moment. All these half-hearted attempts at description are a weak challenge yet a challenge still to the idea that a literature reduced to its virtues would be virtuous. Fairground rides in films and fiction fit so closely to my experience of rides that they rhetorically talk me into thinking there is no such thing as freedom, with the qualification that playing gooseberry isn't always unpaid. Who do we thank for the qualification though, as in what do we do with a get-out clause that turns circular thinking into a spiral?

SET 70

The chances of the lives. The voice choice of fresh-faced bards straight
out of Creation College and other fancy realists, teenage churchgoers,
all comers, gamers, old timers and even *we have to clock-on now* gypsies.
We appreciate though that most people keep almost everyone else's
silence on the boil and any cultural exceptions are worthy of headphones
and a place on the lush syllabus. An alligator don't live here not in the
shadow of this house that's just a chained bike fallen over. The middle
classes graft tattooed violence from skin to skin from alteration on the
job to working tautology from adopted idea to collected nibbles. There
is much skidding of wagon wheels in civilisation tonight. Doctors are
bubbling up in the fountains of Avalon and TV directors are longing to
find a well-used philistine. Curator, guard your reptiles.

To be imperfectly honest one of these set-ups is a bit like reality tv
without the reality but with extra adverts. Less than two minutes of
digital Kerrang and I feel as if I've just dredged up an ancient curse so
switch back to nicam and I'm on that Grumpy Old Men show sawing a
loud dominion into two scraggy mysteries which is the biggest mystery
life or death and why did John Stone have a cardboard flag of Egypt just
because he was born there I was jealous of its jaundiced green I didn't
like my stupid Jack with its dully crayoned triangular impossibility mum
hated it too but she made it for me she said *John's more English than you
are why don't I make you the flag our brave rebels hoisted on the post office* I
felt like a jehovah saying *yes I'll have that blood transfusion* retrospectively.
Each of us brings something to play with such as a crayoned choice-
machine paper nest of numbers and tucked-up colours that said *You
love Miss* but the finger co-ordination fumbled. The morning went on
for hours. An altruistic lunchtime restocked the cupboard with Split by
the Groundhogs. Afternoon ended inspiration. Larkin's poems made
me spit my hair was long my tie was wide my desk-drawer was full of
confiscated pocket-sized trash-treasure.cut sticky corners

Millions hoping to win millions have the chance of winning George
Melly's death-mask and I'm not ungrateful having been a hunt saboteur
for a day a crusty bypass protestor for a day allotting opportunity slots
for retro disguise as an archaeologist takes the opportunity offered by
the Earth's amnesty to hand in his tools.

SET 71

There is a type of writing that bores I couldn't tell you what it is it might be yours get up walk around come back but the type sticks unlike revisiting a beach in the evening trying to feel as you felt earlier instead of enjoying the cool disparity and muted lambency. I love the slant of rain as much as the straight down of rain and my relaxed relationship to rain's indifference is as human as anxiety. Another study of identical twins throws up conflicting results one twin gets top marks for History the other scorches the staircase but astrologers are hypocrites when pope and royal come out on the baloney balcony they chant their square-bashed cheer along with the rest of the urban zoo—a prophetic weld equidistant between Woolf's lighthouse and a runny third eye. Such writing, when served up as poetry, is a fake junkie, just another low-risk opinion a deputy taking the heat but on expenses. Unverifiable association flirts.

Only when pitching the tent do you believe the world isn't flat. Discharging Tibet of blame for how hilly high it is. What a flattering thing language is. Totemic autopsy.

Went around the back of the church to where church and church hall are identical looking for the door to the jumble sale. The nonconformist temple cellar leads to the attic via rites so mundane they reek of damp hermetics. Lose yourself in these unrealised patterns and you will soon be found. The church and its halls take up the whole block this door has had a lick of rust the railings drip from the bottom up the windows crawl with cunning blind gothic. Gave them bin bags full of beanbags and some other stuff including a strimmer.go ear to ground

The Basil Brush pencil case was tempting. Felt sick had to sit down on the shopping mall bench and watch parrots in waistcoats conjurers barbecued on scrap metal and beautifully mutilated moths walk by on their way to a spanking new ENT department half way up the mountain between Dr. Ho's empty hermitage being interviewed by Michael Palin and the Leningrad Hermitage reflected in the lake below. I hope you don't mind me calling it Leningrad like most of the avant-garde I need to adjust to a life without progress. Fiddled books fall off the back of the dustcart. An anagram approaching light-speed.

SET 72

Going round the kitchen singing George Michael in the manner of Ethel Merman is soon spent fuel then it's singing Morrissey in the manner of Kenneth McKellar then leaving the chore unfinished to go and record this. *Dad, do you want an A to Z of Leicester* and for a moment I actually ask myself the same question to which the answer is inevitably *no* but I wish it wasn't. A fan liked my use of *wreckers' logic* in this *packet of reckless inventor's sea-leg insurance* but I wasn't asked if that's what it really was my container was assumed into safety simultaneously with the Virgin Mary and that made it difficult to experience it fully. I can read Gertrude Stein now that being browned-off by boring opinion and pop poetry make social life as hard as asking *what have the Americans done for us* in the present climate in my stomach. Getting old and intolerant of experience makes us think we should have published a life's work when we were young. The noise in the bar demands a boxer's defence then steely silence booms through the door beyond which the street is quietly drinking the rain. Kenny will like that line probably the only one who does. Flat banter goes on practising its moonlight planting its magnetic hedge around the edge of *coincidence*.

The tenure is captured. Separate claims. Change demands change.

Vegetables are not foolish vegetables are not wise a heavenly body the old man had been looking at all his life suddenly left the universe it didn't just fade away. Always knew the spiel about computers wouldn't feed Africa it would be funny if it did and not surreal at all. The teacher in the classroom furthest from reception found herself locked in with the class while everyone else evacuated for the fire drill she looked in the gaps between box files to find a way-out-atlas but alas panic is logical in illogical scenarios and fear the coincidental worst-case of the *other's* death book squeezed into a text where a birth should be. In her sports car she asked *do you like Tom Petty* as she fiddled with the dial and *coincidentally* I did.gulf clobber

A roundabout is not the same shape as a jaw dribbling spaghetti but I went round one once that was a wishbone and in the centre was a karaoke pub where local councillors went to relax forming the most unlikely spontaneous duets with people who don't even know what the Council do but *coincidentally* know the words to the same songs.

SET 73

Reverting to a strictly pampered childhood deceased kings try to play wife-swap but god corpses get in the way. Heraldic demon don't bite. The indifferent meat of muses shushing each other in the library. Having danced my way around the world my joints are achingly free of adolescence oh no an army of pre-Raphaelites are sweeping this way shall I hide myself by swooping into the actions of a dandy? Judas set a good example. Alfred Jarry set out his stall on Wembley Way selling blue but nothing else was blue, not even Barthes. Barthes was on What's My Line none of the panel got it.

Always do best when doing something else instead. Never had to deal with German troops but I had to teach Simon Armitage I've dealt with what German troops wrote with more confidence. The Supermarket had everything but it didn't have a burnt-out watch repairer jealous of a jewellery counter. Tried telling my Head that these story tellers doing creative week in the classroom and the rounds of crèche tents at festivals are passé reactionaries who don't give a toss but he didn't give one either it was a job and it got it done. How long does it take to make a judgement minutes or centuries and if an editor inserts a narrator into the narrative I have to wonder forty years later why anyone actually needs an egg-timer but they perform their task as a socialising gift it's grandchildren's feelings that count in grandparents' thoughts.press home

The coach tour carrying a community of strangers stopped where Steve could serendipitally say this is where John Lennon is buried at *the place of the mutilated horse* and sure enough the bones of a horse are scattered here around a shrine shaped like Yoko's silhouette but overhearing him the tour guide confidently informs us the bones are not actually buried here in the middle of scenic nowhere but rest piecemeal in a dry-dock in Portsmouth. In dreams there is a forensic gathering you stand there and the world arranges itself around you a greenhouse erected around tombstones opens up as a coffee house where a ship's cook cultivates orchids which he photographs and sends to the *places to go and things to do* brochures which hence become birthday cards for the illiterate. You have to admit that this is narrative even if not your favourite one to take to bed. A tourist kisses anyone and anything convinces himself the partisans fighting at the gates of the football ground love freedom as much as he hates small change.

SET 74

Exploring the various pieces of Victoriana left strategically behind by a Victorian explorer isn't fresh enough even for the virgin young. A small Baltic state that never existed and never will issues passports stamped *If you want topical we've got topical If you want tropical go south* and such straight talking goes down a treat even when descending into the most labyrinthine digestive system. Daft musicians who believe their eerie music mimics the extra-terrestrial actually argue about it for moral support no don't laugh at what musicians write with the same tears through which you read such hormonal politics - two bored hotel night-shifters in reception discussing reception theory are sewers with no sewage. By the way the bank statement I pulled from the hole in the wall in the state bank of the Baltic state that isn't there said *Geology is wholly dependent upon personality* but personality is dependant on the clapometer.the band played crap but their autographs flourished

I stared without care at the chain on the bear with his chin on the chair staring at air. Apples burnt onto the tree by the autumn flamethrower. Internationalism is tempting.

The days pass including the secularised ones. It could be said and indeed it has that children go into school on their first day at school and leave school on their last day at school. What passed in the days in-between is nobody's business. In the middle of a civil war the lazy soldier fights as hard as the busy businessman and it might even be his latent energy that turns the battle on a crude decision though probably not. The Death of Zen impressed the full-house and the same the next night and the next the box office installed more phones the play moved up west. My social experiment would be similar to teenage behaviour like walking around with the hood on your hoodie down when its raining and up when it stops but the results would be different because these gay sciences are only perverse when set against their own examples. Astronaut returns bloated with pride but gets prodded and poked and nothing seems funny or important to him any more. The same might be said of a writer from the 60s cryogenically holed-up for forty years disorienting himself into the hotel lobby then walking up to strangers and asking them if they happen to be current influences on his old prose style. Only a Goth couple oozing morality bother to reply.

SET 75

Exciting new religions arrive by mail order because they haven't been ordered. It is difficult to choose between them do I go for an expensive one because it's free or a cheap one in case there's a follow-through on the phone? All unnecessary repetition is a throwback to a self long since lost for words. An opera from the *colonies* doesn't look lost for words the stage production is rich as only those brought up in true poverty can be unembarrassed by the proud display of shared achievement. R.D. Laing is clinging to the ivy that clings to the house I can't tell if he is climbing up and in or down and out I could be Jonathan Harker and he could be Dracula and this could be a diary of unspeakable scholarship not just a self-conscious question and answer session concluding a banal lecture *Have we any final questions yes you there at the back the only one who hasn't said anything yet why did you bother coming surely you didn't just want to listen that would be too shyly working-class and yes yes speak up please what's that does our guest believe there can be such a thing as a modern fairy tale?* The guest speaker must be Marina Warner then I only came because my mate fancies her but he seems to have slipped away leaving me feeling as if I could be classed as a small country even though it seems pretty big to me like Wales.

The deepest grottoes are wedged away in this ivy green humid cleft in this dripping damp valley each has a regulated mirage of Our Lady of all Parricides but torn up page 3's and tabloids blemish the bliss however the scraps of newspaper are real the photographs though creased are of real people and the news though old is a fair record. The images steaming down the rocks on the other visionary hand are only captured shadows. The supplicant on his knees is asking for the keys the universally known metonymic ritual of anything that rattles the goings-on up at the big 'ouse. *I bought you tickets for the waterfall and you poured away all the change* were Pete Brown's words but the way Jack Bruce sung them showed chimerical understanding.

River you don't need to go on for miles and miles. Dazzling sherbet river you don't need to do anything you are sweet modern and crambo complete.mocking salute

The modesty of the prodigy never fooled the fool.

SET 76

The right-wing libertarian pooh-poohing all our concerns pays for his heart surgery with our money he is put to sleep by a poem about a used-car salesman written by a woman who has never even met a used-car salesman no matter waking and forgetting what you were dreaming what about what you were thinking being superseded by two hermaphrodite wrestlers flashing in and out of being beautiful and giving birth. The winner gets to eat the loser's husband. I couldn't come up with anything better. I've never met anyone. I wouldn't dream of putting people I've met into a word-cage but I might dream it. I didn't support the miner's strike 100% because of global warming how's that for an exotic political position? I supported the miners 99%. Caught out.

Man-on-stilts tries to board ferry for the first and last time too tidy a stunt for a genius maybe the genie is running out of steam the opposite of Charlie Watts on Top of the Pops going down with the ship his sailor's cap sardonically atilt then submerged in bubbles. Bring the world up-to-date—chip away the tears of glue. Two cousins play Confession in a photographer's darkroom and Communion with one of his albino biscuits they are soul hopping they grow up to be expert soul hoppers but will never understand why the more mean-spirited the letters are in the local paper the more obscure are the class contradictions but of course a judge pretends to understand especially when issuing his cruel glee of multiple life sentences. We had better take a crash course in New Criticism. Coat smashed.organised like a body

The right-wing libertarian is an inexperienced sphinx.

Ireland measured against Duchamp's *Stoppages* but what of it?

Hermit's dress-sense and fashion designer's self-hate *these are a few of my favourite* malts echoing through chronic teenage surrealism. Dusk— the Settings discuss with Judge John Deed why the turning point in the narrow country road makes them think of a puritan having an apparition. Subjects such as the layering of reality through fictional representation invite themselves and their pals to the palace party though the places at table are already set with needle and nail-scissors. The Borrowers discuss the combustible properties of the apparition independent of its borrowed subject, soot.

I do not agree or disagree with the argument that too many students are entering university in the UK today I do not agree or disagree with the argument that more students should be able to receive a university education in the UK today because the terms of both assertions are unmanned terminals I don't just believe in free education I believe that people should be free without it and free for it you can take your exams you can take your exams and screw them screw 'em to the door of the police station be resistance fighters here and now but don't get caught or they'll vivisect your laughter and force-feed you prosodic waste from a novel chocka with so many homeless characters refusing to cooperate with the authorities that their cardboard rubbish is mutating into Superman's last supper of *prime evil* soup so no matter how emotionally militant I'm not really talking about an anarchy with or without postage stamps with or without a head of state in national costume no this is not talking it's not even writing in the usual sense as all excuses have been abandoned except for those saved-up Dadaist analgesics knocked-back because the poetry elves sitting on the shelves are more needy and numerous than the complete set of *Colemanballs* sharing a shelf with campsite guides and maps of National Parks yes there really is more unrhymed verse than commentators' balls-ups but that's not necessarily healthy when an elf gets heavy with horsemeat its shadow a lighter self altogether could be the ingredients in your own RTA sandwich escaping from the wreckage like a taste of a miniaturised library with large-print cookbook sticking out at all angles into the illiterate sky where an intimate banjo sunset is sacked like the book depository in old Alexandria by sky divers dropping in to check form then hanging about while the classics swell up with the rain some as large as sheep sheering the gooseberry green pasture of its texture and separating it from the taste of greengage for an accountable analogy would involve world and language in some sort of combo made up of a stamp collector a train spotter a job-lot of qualifications and a proof reader but not in any order that would add-up to a text not in the way a gooseberry is made of text but we don't need to be told that the unembarrassed government of breeze can cool the lizard of unfair laissez-faire lyric 'cause I've enjoyed myself but some people need a literary agent not just in order to sleep but in order to elect the correct dreams whereas I've no inkling what an expertly picked bona fide ambition could be because when I found a fresh bone in a packet of old suggestions it was a natural anomaly.stilted stilts

Setting Examples (watching an advertisement after reading the book)

What claustrophobic line has the agoraphobic poet put his autistic arse on / he is surely the son of a moving group / over sensitive identities and billboard tautology / the soil burns / inside every egg is a piece of suicidal nonsense trying to get out / machine-gunning the tropes / a trace, a footfall, an approved school / Those stains are your eyes / This compass is too steady to be working properly / conversation dries up in the naturalistic novel / my sense of injustice grew into a mystery / leaks a séance / Capitalism would have saved me had it known I was there / the cleaners, all mothers of Beatles, arrive / a fish leaps out of the river and swallows a cow / look at that isn't it interesting in fact it's quite moving / second-hand oracle / you go in quick you establish the Danelaw you get out again / tracksuits are not part of the ecosystem / We await preservative / learn how to draw and dress teddybear / Education has an audience / .jesus was pasted to the cross / out of harm's way in the dungeon of a bouncy castle / Mother Nature threatened my best friend / a passport photo taken in Pangaea / we only went to Eden to buy money / What a wagging tongue you have there Mr. Thesaurus / fog diced and displayed like fudge in a shop window / I've never found the romantics particularly romantic / a sentimental horror, an unstable skill / living a literal life not a literary one / I can't be named Wafer Moth for nothing / laying desperate eggs of sorrow in the middle of the road / beneath which a witch migraine twitches / we dropped names into the harbour / Underwaterwear left under bushes was never plural / chewing gum and its descendants / the Iraqi's chest was splattered through by his free kick / mannerly saluting fascist in the shower to rinse underarm / a rusting lyre half submerged in a fake lake / from the slave trade to Smash Hits / cherry picked biographeme / The sky is the colour of thin cucumber / Unimaginable guilt at what we're excluding from a multiple viewpoint / the physically ill and the mentally ill battle it out / a generation of palindromes / A sloshing index / The longer the tramp looks at me the more he appears to recognise himself / A community's mixed feelings about its joy riders / skirmish echoecho phosphorescent atrophy / chaperone pedantic little truths past distant galaxies of deception / drawing of an insolvent octopus spread across a billiard table / from adopted idea to collected nibbles / Gave them bin bags full of beanbags / singing Morrissey in the manner of Kenneth McKellar / muses shushing each other in the library / personality is dependant on the clapometer / River you don't need to go on for miles

Setting the Vessel on a Trestle (author's afterword)

I set out to produce poems in which the density of poetic thinking would be balanced by tonal lightness. To do this I needed language compacted into blocks yet leavened by careless directness. I wanted to say a few things too, not necessarily important things, I just wanted to create a process through which the saying of anything would be pleasurable. The real, the imaginary, the memory: these are interchangeable categories in my poetics. Opinion, politics, postmodern *truth*: these are movable targets for the peculiarity of the artform. The Settings became a vehicle of framed opportunity in which I wanted it possible to maintain a sense of freedom while focussing on the control of the unconscious particular. Each Set is an artificial context, one in which it becomes easy to *say things* in a way similar to normal careless thought processes while being different because such processes are not usually framed, not usually concentrated to such a degree before being *strung along* by language. The *saying* is real, by which I mean the *writing* is real, but it may become unreal (in the common-sense notion of unreal) through the medium itself i.e. the poetry act takes the real and turns it into something unreal. I am not sure how this relates to Robert Creeley's poetics; I was reading him heavily at the time and there was a connection but how much of that carried through is debatable.

The Settings were first written in the early 00s. By the time of the second Iraqi War I was up to Set 54. Many were written one summer when I was in pain and discomfort following an infection picked up in an operation and I typed away in an attempt to think about something else. I am not sure where the original set of procedural rules came from but each Set was to be just over half a page of A4 with one paragraph concluded by a tagged on phrase following immediately behind the full stop. Out of the final 77 Sets one has this quirk missing, on purpose of course. Part of the original project included writing some mock, or actual, philosophical meander into each text but this became less conscious as the things progressed, becoming almost naturalised by the contextual process. As for subject, there was no intention of writing about anything particular—what came would come, and it did. The fact that a few themes insisted their way through became more apparent at the revision stage but these themes were neither cut nor expanded, just left to float. Neither was there any attempt at relating one Set to another; they are discrete poems, though siblings obviously.

I said when being interviewed by Andrew Duncan (*Don't Start Me Talking,* Salt 2006) that the Settings were not prose poems or that if they were then they were bad ones. When the idea was first conceived I had in mind a kind of anti-prose-poem that would look and smell like one but give a different taste and have a different texture. One way of doing this was by making the conclusion of each Set flat and deflationary, almost deliberately poor in the sense that they never approached closure, either artificially or in actuality (i.e. it would not be a matter of simply having occluded conclusions—the lack of closure *was* actual), and yet as they increased in number a weird kind of closure began to seep in, while still maintaining the skewed balance I was aiming for. Two bouts of revision tended to round this off and smooth the jaggedness of the originals into something that looks a lot more like conventional prose poetry but these things are relative and I find the finished result charmingly deceptive—I still do not consider them as prose poetry. A prose poem is a single entity whereas each Set is an arrangement that uses the unit of the paragraph to set apparently unrelated (poetically & idea-wise) acts of saying together and against each other. However, they are not collage either, they are not placings or insertions, they are organic and sequential, despite the disruptions or displacements. Therefore, to my mind, each Set is a poem in the ordinary sense, not a prose poem. There is nothing particularly original in this regard either, as there are numerous examples in current North American innovative poetry that are not prose poems or poetic prose in the accepted sense, but to be honest I am not particularly fussed if a reader wants to call these pieces prose poems—I'm just *saying*.

Tim Allen (September 2007)

SET NOTES (INC. ACKNOWLEDGEMENTS)

NOTE: Some of the following might seem unnecessary but I am always surprised by the partiality of cultural references, how names we take for granted in the circle of our own interests can be completely unknown by others. It is also highly probable that many references here will mean nothing to those not familiar with British TV. If you want to find out more then Google away.

Set 1. *Argyle* – Plymouth Argyle Football Club. *Norman* – Norman Jope, friend and Plymouth poet. *Eternal Return* – Concept of Frederick Nietzsche's.

Set 2. *Sailors fighting in the dancehall* – 'Life on Mars' by David Bowie. *Union Street* – Street in Plymouth famous in Naval circles for its nightlife. *Steven Hawking* – The physicist / cosmologist. *Jack Hawkins* – British actor fitted with a voice box following throat surgery. *Screamin' Jay Hawkins* – Early American Rock 'n Roller, loved particularly by English rockers such as Screaming Lord Sutch and Viv Stanshall.

Set 3. *Pincher Martin* – Novel by William Golding.

Set 5. *Co-op* – The Co-operative Society, once believed in socialist shopping. *Alice in Sunderland* – Graphic novel by Bryan Talbot. *Attila the Stockbroker* – Performance poet / musician. *Stalin Malone* – song by *Elvis* Costello.

Set 6. *The Silver Sword* – Children's book by Ian Serraillier, serialised on TV in late 50s. *The tide is high . . .* – 'The Tide is High' by Blondie. *Debbie* Harry.

Set 7. *Weymouth Pier* – Weymouth, seaside town in Dorset where I went to school. The pier disappeared a long time ago.

Set 8. *prog rock* – Progressive Rock Music; popular in late 60s & early 70s.

Set 9. *Breton* – André Breton (1896–1966); French poet & polemicist, leader of the Surrealists.

Set 10. *David* – David Cox, close friend through my childhood and adolescence. *Michaux* – Henri Michaux (1899–1984), French poet / artist. *Sean O'Brien* – English poet, bullish negative critic of anything smacking of avant-garde. *Sean Bonney* – English poet, militantly anti-mainstream. *Motion* – Andrew Motion, the Poet Laureate.

Set 12. *Alice* – Alice Cooper, the Rock Star. *Portland* – Isle of Portland, Dorset, UK, where I was brought up.

Set 13. *Robert Creeley* (1926–2005) – American modernist poet. *Duffy* – Carol Ann Duffy, British poet. (The occasion was a poetry reading in which these two very different poets shared star billing.)

Set 14. *Lorna Doone* – Eponymous heroine in the novel by R.D. Blackmore. *Maureen Lipman* – English actress. *Jack K* – Jack Kerouac.

Set 15. *The Toppers* – Female dance troupe v. pop. on early TV variety shows.

Set 16. *Devonport* – Area of Plymouth famous for its Naval Dockyard.

Set 17. *Cardinal Newman* – Catholic Teachers' Training College named after the 19c. Cardinal (I failed the interview). *Dom Joly* – English comedian, known for 'Trigger Happy TV'.

Set 18. *Arvon Foundation* – Creative Writing residence. *Steve* – Steve Spence, friend and Plymouth poet. *John Kinsella* – Australian poet, founder of the innovative poetry publisher Salt. *Mencius* – Chinese Confucian philosopher (371–289 BC). *Stride* – poetry imprint run by Rupert Loydell.

Set 19. *the school the train passes* – Drake Primary School, Plymouth, I taught there for 14 years (Brenda, my wife, still works there). *Calstock* – Small town on the banks of the Tamar.

Set 21. *Lost Jockey* – *The Lost Jockey*, painting by Magritte and recurring motif.

Set 22. *Ballard* – J.G. Ballard, British author. *Danelaw* – area of Anglo-Saxon England ruled by the Danes from 9th to 11th centuries. *John Digby* – Surreal artist and poet. *Dan Dare* – Character from Children's comic Eagle. *Paul Nash* (1889–1946) – English neo-surrealist artist.

Set 23. *Connect 4* – A game. *Kenny* – Kenny Knight, friend and Plymouth poet. *Jeff Nuttall* – What happened to the heroes? *Alan and Geraldine* – Alan Halsey and Geraldine Monk, premier innovative English poets.

Set 24. *The Cantos* – by Ezra Pound (1885–1972). *Robert Smith* – British musician/singer with The Cure. *Fat Bob* – what the music press used to call him. *Glastonbury* – the music festival held near Glastonbury, Somerset, UK.

Set 25. *Tamaritan* – The Tamaritans, am-dram company in Plymouth. *Ford Princess* – a car in the 70s (If not please don't bother telling me). *Dali* – Beautiful town in Kunming Province, S.W. China. *Bataille* – Georges Bataille (1897–1962), French writer.

Set 26. *Terrible Work* – Poetry magazine edited by the author 1993–2000. Now a website. *Arthur Scargill* – Militant left-wing leader of the N.U.M. at the time of the miners' strike. *Mandelson* – Peter Mandelson, New Labour politician.

Set 27. *Mark Thatcher* – Son of Margaret Thatcher (got lost in the desert, but bad luck meant they found the waster). *Douglas Bader* – famous

WW2 pilot with prosthetic legs. *Rimbaud* – Arthur Rimbaud (1854–1891), French symbolist poet, became gun-runner in Africa (Also lost a leg.). *Tom Raworth* – Rather extraordinary British poet. *Babbage* – Charles Babbage, pioneering computer boffin.

Set 28. *Peter Redgrove* (1932–2003) – English poet. *Boots & Saddles* – 50s TV series about US cavalry fighting Indians in Arizona. *BNP* – British National Party, extreme right-wing political party. *NME* – *New Musical Express*, rock-music newspaper. *Room 101* – British TV programme in which guests choose things they hate to be symbolically swept from the face of the Earth, introduced by comedian Paul Merton. *Inspector Frost* – TV detective played by David Jason. *The Black & White Minstrels* – Song & dance TV variety show infamous for its blacked-up faces.

Set 29. *Cronenberg* – David Cronenberg, American film director (*Crash* etc.).

Set 30. *the rain falls gently* . . . – Guillaume Apollinaire (1880–1918), from one of his *Calligrammes*. *Lostwithiel* – Cornish market town. *Tony Harrison* – English poet from Leeds known for his colloquial idiom in classic forms.

Set 31. *Pavlov* (1849–1936) – Russian behavioural psychologist, famous for his 'dog'.

Set 32. *Never Mind the Buzzcocks* – British TV comedy quiz show featuring guests from the world of Pop and Rock. Named after seminal punk band.

Set 33. *Miss Dalton* – Kate Dalton, a teaching colleague of mine in Plymouth. *Olson* – Charles Olson (1910–1970), American modernist poet.

Set 34. *Pastoral* – Beethoven's Pastoral Symphony. *The Byrds* – Best American band ever. *Heidegger* (1889–1976) – The German philosopher.

Set 35. *Ch ch changes* – Changes by David Bowie. *Carl Perkins* – Early country-rocker. *Moorcock* – Michael Moorcock, British SF/fantasy writer.

Set 36. *Howlin' Wolf* & *Robert Johnson* – seminal blues musicians. *I Get Around* – Big hit for the Beach Boys. *Pangaea* – the original single continent.

Set 37. *a little nervous laughter* – From 'Feel It' by Kate Bush.

Set 38. *The Piper at the Gates of Dawn* – First album by Pink Floyd/Syd Barrett.

Set 40. *Fortuneswell* – Street on Portland. *Jarvis Cocker* – Singer with Pulp. *Dune* – SF novel.

Set 42. *Königsberg & Kaliningrad* – are the same Russian (once German) city. *Lorca* – Federico García Lorca (1898–1936), the great Spanish poet murdered by Fascists.

Set 43. *Observer book* – Observer's Books: children's information and spotter books.

Set 44. *John Wilkinson* – Avant-garde British poet. *Etc. Dreams* – What poet and friend Wendy Ruthroff and I called our performing collaborations.

Set 45. *The High Numbers* – What The Who were called for brief period before fame. *Angela Carter* (1940–1992) – Gothically-inclined British author.

Set 46. *Desmond Morris* – Author of *The Naked Ape* etc, also a surrealist painter.

Set 47. *Animal Farm* – By George Orwell (1903–1950). *Myra Hindley* – one of the two Moors Murderers. *Green Goddess* – Army fire engines, brought in during firemen's strikes etc.

Set 49. *Carry On Filming* – The *Carry On* films, cheeky Brit comedy. *News Night* – Long-running late night news programme on British TV. *Big Issue* – Magazine sold by homeless on British high streets.

Set 50. *Ed Dorn* (1929–1999)– American poet. *Craig Raine* – British poet (Ed, unlike everyone else associated with modernist & innovative poetry, had a liking for Raine's work). *Potteries* – The Five Towns, Stoke-on-Trent. *The cathedral* – In Cobh, Co. Cork, Ireland, where my mother came from. *Rousseau* – Henri Rousseau (1844–1910), French naïve painter. *Blake* – William Blake (1757–1827), English poet/artist.

Set 51. *Adrian Mitchell* – British socialist/populist poet. *Pete Brown* – English musician/songwriter/poet; wrote lyrics for Cream. *Andrew Duncan* – English poet/editor. *Heinz* – Two-hit-wonder 60s pop star, protégé of Joe Meek (see Set 55). *Jet Harris* – original bass-player in The Shadows.

Set 52. *Braden Gang* – The Bradens were a large family of boys on a rival council estate on Portland when I was a kid. We were scared of their myth. *Heaney's Blackberries* – Seamus Heaney's poem 'Blackberry Picking'. *Mark Wallinger* – British conceptual artist. *Muldoon* – Paul Muldoon, Irish poet.

Set 53. *Tess* – *Tess of the D'Urbervilles* by Thomas Hardy. *Man Ray* – Surrealist photographer.

Set 54. *Altered Images* – Scottish pop-punk band fronted by Claire Grogan. *Blair-Bush* – monstrous hybrid creature.

Set 55. *Compact & Harpers* – Early-60s sitcoms on British T.V. *John Leyton* – Actor turned pop star with No. 1 hit *Johnny Remember Me* produced by legendary English record-producer *Joe Meek*. *NT* – The National Trust. *NUT* – The National Union of Teachers. *Roland Penrose* – English surrealist artist and aristocrat, one-time husband of *Lee Miller*, American photographer, model and surrealist muse. *AA & RAC* – the two British motoring organisations.

Set 56. *Millbrook* – Small town in S.E. Cornwall, on opposite side of Tamar to Plymouth. *Cardinal Spelman & Spiro Agnew* – Respectively, right wing American-Irish cardinal and politician who I happen to be related to. *Fast Show* – Comedy sketch show on British T.V.

Set 57. *Foucault* – Michael Foucault (1926–1984), French philosopher. *Which* – consumer guide magazine. *Hinge & Bracket* – English musical comedy duo. *Smash Hits* – long running teenage pop magazine. *Woodlands & Crealy Adventure Park* – Adventure parks in Devon, UK.

Set 58. *The Smiths* – Best English band, ever.

Set 59. *Brenda* – Brenda Allen.

Set 60. *Hopkins* – Gerard Manley Hopkins (1844–1889), English poet *Hughes* – Ted Hughes (1930–1998), English poet. *Stanislaw Lem* – Polish S.F. writer. (If you have never heard of him then perhaps you have heard of the film *Solaris*; he wrote the book)

Set 61. *Tanguy* – Yves Tanguy (1900–1955), French surrealist painter. *Richard Dawkins* – English evolutionary biologist, famous for his polemics against religion. *Georgie Best* – George Best, N. Irish footballer.

Set 62. *The Group* – Group of influential English poets who used to meet under the guidance of Philip Hobsbaum from late 50s to mid 60s. *Morley* through to *Whiteread* – Some winners of the Turner Prize. *The Merseybeats* – English 60s pop group, 'Suspicion' was one of their hits.

Set 63. *younger than that now* – 'Forever Young' by Bob Dylan.

Set 64. *Paul Celan* (1920–1970) – Jewish gnomic and experimental poet born in Romania, wrote mostly in German.

Set 65. *John Ashbery* – American modernist poet. *Tom Jones* – the singer & book.

Set 66. *Bergson* – Henri Bergson (1859–1941), French philosopher. *Dave* – See Set 10. *Ken Edwards* – Innovative English poet and publisher (Reality Street Editions).

Set 67. *Chapman Brothers* – English conceptual artists.

Set 68. *St. Trinians* – Fictional girls boarding school in comedy films of same name. *Zig Zag Wanderer* – Song by Captain Beefheart. *Rapido* – A board game. *Casualty* – Hospital soap on British T.V.

Set 70. *Kerrang!* – Heavy metal mag and radio station. *Grumpy Old Men* – British T.V. programme in which celebrity oldsters grump about modern life. *John Stone* – Childhood friend. *Split* – classic heavy rock album by British band *The Groundhogs*. *George Melly* (1926–2007) – George did everything.

Set 71. *Virginia Woolf* (1882–1941) – English novelist. *Basil Brush* – My favourite puppet. *Dr. Ho* – Doctor of Chinese medicine interviewed by one-time Python *Michael Palin* on his China series. (Dr. Ho gave me a cup of tea.)

Set 72. *George Michael* – British pop star. *Ethel Merman* – American actress/ singer. *Morrissey* – British singer, formerly of The Smiths. *Kenneth McKellar* – Scottish singer of the 50s and early 60s. *Gertrude Stein* (1874–1946) – American modernist writer. *Tom Petty* – American rockstar.

Set 73. *Alfred Jarry* (1873–1907) – French writer, the creator of Ubu & Pataphysics. *Barthes* – Roland Barthes (1915–1980), French semiologist and writer. *Simon Armitage* – English poet.

Set 75. *R.D. Laing* (1927–1989)– Scottish psychiatrist/writer, famous for his anti-psychiatry therapy and theories. *Jonathan Harker* – Character in Bram Stoker's *Dracula*. *Marina Warner* – English writer, known for her explorations of myth. *Pete Brown* – See Set 51. *Jack Bruce* – Scottish rock & jazz musician, bass guitarist/singer with Cream.

Set 76. *Charlie Watts* – Drummer with The Rolling Stones. *Duchamp* – Marcel Duchamp (1887–1968), avant-garde French artist; his *Stoppages* had a weird influence on me years ago. *Judge John Deed* – Eponymous character in TV series.

Set 77. *Colemanballs* – An annual collection of hilarious commentators' mistakes compiled by *Private Eye* (I am always given one on Christmas Day).

Printed in the United Kingdom
by Lightning Source UK Ltd.
134887UK00002B/154-165/P